A Praying Life™

LEARNING TO PRAY IN A DISTRACTING WORLD

LEADER'S MANUAL

WRITTEN BY PAUL E. MILLER

*Dedicated to the memory of my father, Jack Miller,
who not only taught me the importance and value
of prayer, but also modeled it with his life.*

enter His story

The mission of seeJesus is to help people see and reflect the life, death, and resurrection of Jesus through our discipleship resources and training.

We design, write, and market Bible curriculum (study guides, books, videos) for small groups within the church for both evangelism and discipleship, to reach a postmodern world that is increasingly secular and a church that is increasingly untaught.

As a non-profit organization we rely upon the support and gifts of faithful friends. We appreciate your prayers and financial support. If you would like to contribute financially to our ministry, you may do so through any of the following means:

PHONE: 1-866-JesusNet (1-866-537-8763)
Monday through Friday, 8:00 - 5:00 Eastern Time

MAIL: (Make checks payable to seeJesus)
seeJesus
P.O. Box 197
Telford PA, 18969

WEBSITE: www.seeJesus.net

COVER DESIGN: Seth Guge
INTERIOR DESIGN & LAYOUT: Carol Smith
COPY EDITOR: Lori Mitchell
SCRIPTURE EDITOR: Lydia Leggett

TABLE OF CONTENTS

1. Why is Prayer So Hard? 5

2. Becoming a Child of Your Father 15

3. Begin Early With Your Father....................23

4. "Helplessness", the Key to Effective Praying 27

5. Ask Your Father Anything 35

6. Entering Your Father's Story Through Prayer.......... 47

7. Learning to Listen to Your Father....................57

8. Put the Word to Work 63

9. Prayer Work 69

10. Thanking God.....................................73

11. Repentance and Intercessory Praying..................... 75

Appendix A: Scripture for your cards 79

Appendix B 83

Appendix C 91

About the Author....................................93

TEACHING NOTES:

Throughout the manual you will see Paul Miller's teaching notes. These notes only appear in the Leader's Manual. They will be formatted in *a lighter color and italicized* so that you can easily identify them from the rest of the manual text.

The notes will help you fill in the details if there are any questions or if you want to review the material ahead of time.

The notes represent Paul's most recent teaching notes, so do not follow precisely the original notes from the video. Occasionally there is additional material.

In the Participant's manual, individual points within each lesson may not always fall on the same page as the Leader's manual. The lessons themselves always start and end on the same page.

ACKNOWLEDGMENT:

Dr. David Powlison, served as theological advisor and reviewer of this *A Praying Life* study. He teaches counseling at Westminster Theological Seminary and edits the *Journal of Biblical Counseling*. At the end of each lesson, Dr. Powlison has added some additional reflections of his own.

LESSON ONE

WHY IS PRAYER SO HARD?

Or, "How do I pray when my own prayers put me to sleep?"

This lesson is much better if you teach the first half of the lesson yourself. To do this, first watch the video to see Paul's interactions with the group. Copy Paul's approach by having the group do the five minute prayer time and ask the questions yourself. Do this only for Points 1 and 2. You can then play the video for Points 3 and 4. Tell them to wait to open their A Praying Life manuals until you've finished the brainstorming at the beginning of Point 1.

 I. GROUP PRAYER ASSIGNMENT: Pray for five minutes—quietly in your seats.

Don't tell them you are going to discuss this assignment or tell them the purpose of the assignment ahead of time. That spoils the effect. Don't do any teaching on prayer prior to this five minute prayer time. It will feel a little awkward, but don't worry about that.

GROUP DISCUSSION:
(This is the Main Question. Stay on it for 5-10 minutes.)

Q. For some of you, that might have been a positive time, but for most Christians, prayer is hard. I want to focus on the negative, even though it might have been positive for some of you. What was hard for you about that five minute prayer time?

(Additional Follow-Up Questions.)

Q. How long was that? How long did it seem?

Q. Who wondered how long this was going to go on for?

Q. What was hard about it?

Q. How many people's minds wandered?

Q. What did it wander to? (List what they say.)

Q. Who felt guilty they couldn't pray well?

RESPONSES FROM A CHURCH IN RICHMOND TO:
"What was your five minute prayer time like?"
- I thought a lot about myself.
- I prayed 3 minutes and daydreamed 2 minutes.
- It felt like ten minutes.
- Hard to stay focused.
- Is 5 minutes up yet?"
- Overwhelming.
- No physical voice responding.
- Hard to be still.

- Feels futile…it may not happen.
- I don't want to pray for what I really want.
- Hard to be silent.
- Fell asleep.
- How do I distinguish my thoughts from God's?
- If I haven't prayed, catching up is overwhelming.
- I feel like a failure.
- Feels like a chore.
- Do I need to say things in the right order?

GROUP DISCUSSION (CONT.):

Q. Let's expand our question by examining problems with prayer in general. What is hard for you about prayer in general, or having a prayer life, or any aspect of prayer?

RESPONSE FROM OTHER CHURCHES ANSWERING THE SAME QUESTION. (You are not alone!)

Church in Williamsburg:
- Mind floats. Is that praying?
- How do you connect with a Spirit?
- Can I pray for what I want? How do I know if it's your will?
- Requires faith.
- Why pray when you can work?
- Feels like I'm praying to a Spiritual being who doesn't want to talk with me.
- Active oriented culture. Hard to slow down.
- Hard to concentrate, to stay focused. The day's to-do list pops up as soon as I slow down.
- He knows it already? Why bore God? Sounds like nagging.
- I like to have a conversation but I don't hear a voice. It's like I'm talking to myself. How's He listening? So hard to concentrate.

- Prayer is boring.
- It uncovers our hearts. I don't want to be uncovered.
- I feel too guilty to stop.
- Overwhelming. So much to pray for.
- Prayers aren't answered. My prayers must be wrong. He's not listening to me. Is He there?

CHURCH IN PHILADELPHIA:
- Takes time.
- Feels like one way—I'm doing all the talking.
- Hard to concentrate. I'm in the middle of praying and I go off.
- We're used to being entertained. Prayer isn't entertainment.
- Evil forces/barriers. Satan uses all these things against us.
- Asking. We're used to doing.
- Seems like it should come naturally. It doesn't.
- Don't do it often enough.

CHURCH IN CHICAGO:
- We try to make it academic. Something we'll be graded on. We think, "I didn't do it right."
- I'm pre-occupied with my petitions, not with God's.
- My mind is crowded. Where do I put prayer?
- Spiritual warfare: fantasies, mind wandering.
- You aren't engaged with anything. How do you dialogue with someone you can't see or hear?
- Doesn't seem natural, therefore I don't think it is real.
- "I have to do it," therefore I feel guilty.

> *"There is a dichotomy between our experience of sonship and our belief in sonship."*

II. OUR EXPERIENCE OF SONSHIP

Q. Define Sonship—I'm not hunting for a technical definition. Just what does Sonship mean to you personally?

> 2 COR. 6:18 "I WILL BE A FATHER TO YOU,
> AND YOU WILL BE MY SONS AND DAUGHTERS,
> SAYS THE LORD ALMIGHTY."

You Visit a "Prayer Therapist" to help you with your relationship with God. The therapist asks you,

Q. Tell me about your relationship with your heavenly Father?
You answer in glowing terms of Sonship describing the access they have to God in Sonship.

Q. But what is it like on a day-to-day basis?
Go back and review the chart, paraphrasing their comments as to what prayer is really like. "It is boring to be with my Father." "I don't know if he is listening," etc.

Q. What would you think of someone who talked in glowing terms about his father but had these kinds of things characterized by his or her relationship with their father?
Dysfunctional.

Summary:

III. FIVE THINGS THAT DEFINE GOOD PRAYER
(helpful to know where you are going)

1. Prayer is like a feast (A good party).

> REV. 3:20 "HERE I AM. I STAND AT THE
> DOOR AND KNOCK. IF ANYONE HEARS MY VOICE
> AND OPENS THE DOOR, I WILL COME IN AND
> EAT WITH HIM AND HE WITH ME."

After dinner we push the dishes aside and get coffee or hot chocolate for the kids and just sit and chew the fat. That is what good prayer feels like.

2. Prayer as relationship.

    * *Prayer is not central to New Testament. Jesus is central. Let me explain:*
    * *Prayer is being with a person. It is being with the Father. As I reflect on that time after dinner I don't think about "communication" or "words" I think about my kids and my wife, Jill. I don't think about the activity (talking) but whom I was talking with.*
    * *Not just a conversation, but fellowship with a divine person.*

3. Prayer is connected with every other part of the Christian life.

    Each part affects the other: Repentance, Faith, Suffering, Work, Word, Love.

    Examples of prayer and love:
    * *The more I pray for my kids the more I love them, the more I am able to concentrate on the key needs in their lives.*
    * *The more I love my kids the more I pray for them. My prayers are crucial in their lives.*

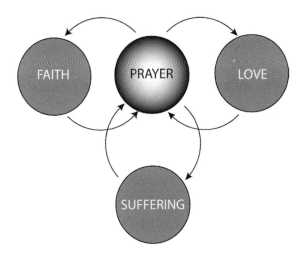

4.   Prayer is a story.

"Through prayer we enter into and learn to see the story that our Father is weaving."

5.   Prayer is an adventure/journey.
   * *Feels like growing up.*
   * *Like learning how to love your husband or your wife or your kids.*
   * *What does that mean? Slow, but steady. Not spectacular, but one of the most important things you do. Not any one thing that makes it happen, but hundreds of little things.*

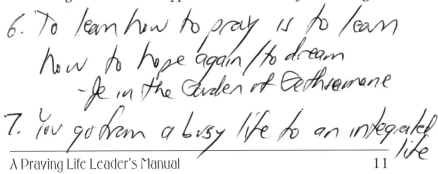

6. To learn how to pray is to learn how to hope again / to dream
   - Je in the Garden of Gethsemane

7. You go from a busy life to an integrated life

IV. THREE CAUTIONS

CAUTION #1: When God begins to give you a rich prayer life—be careful how you talk about it.

* *If you talk too much about what God is doing in your life, it chokes off that prayer life.*
* *In the Sermon on the Mount Jesus has a whole section on being quiet about spirituality in your life. Matt. 6:5-8.*
* *Henri Nouwen compares a rich prayer life to a warm, cozy cabin with a big fire on the hearth on a freezing winter night. But if you talk about your prayer life, it is like leaving with the front door wide open. If you use your relationship with God to make yourself look bigger spiritually, it chokes off that relationship. God is a person. He is sensitive to any form of pride.*
* *"But I might help people." No, the point of prayer is you begin to do things by being quieter. You speak less to people and more to God. Don't turn inner works of God into a show.*

CAUTION #2: We will learn a system in prayer in a later session, but use systems with caution.

* *For example ACTS (Adoration, Confession, Thanksgiving, and Supplication. I write ACTS out) is a shorthand for prayer that has helped many people. But we don't sit down with our wives or husbands and adore them for five minutes, then switch to confession, thank them, and then move to supplication and ask them to take out the trash. Relationships don't work that way.*
* *Since we are made in God's image it's not surprising that he's a lot like us!*
* *You can't manufacture communion with God.*

LESSON ONE: *Why is Prayer So Hard?*

Caution #3: Learning to pray is very possible, but it is not easy, it takes time and aids to learn.

- *Our daughter Kim is bright and cheerful as a person but struggles with motor planning. If she drops a pencil, she has to get up out of the chair walk over to the pencil and lean down and pick it up. She has to think that way because the part of her brain that controls her motor functions doesn't work well.*

- *Jill and I remember Kim teaching herself at six months to turn over. Jill and I watched her for half an hour trying to whip her shoulder around and then follow it with her leg. We do not need a video to remember that. We couldn't help her. If we did, she'd rely on us.*

- *Why say this? We think: "If it's not natural it's not real." Especially in the beginning, prayer is not natural. (This false idea is deep in the American psyche.)*

- *Systems for learning prayer (and we'll learn several) are crucial. They are like wheelchairs or speech computers for the disabled.*

THE LORD'S PRAYER

Jesus taught his disciples to pray because they came to him and said, "Teach us to pray." You can't learn how to pray unless you have a sense of your inability to pray. Lesson 1 is focused on being aware of our inability so we can say with the disciples, "Teach us to pray."

David Powlison's Reflections

Honest prayer also feels like a dire need for help, or like loving someone with all your heart, or like being grateful to someone who does you great good, or like a fear of offending someone whose opinion matters very much, or like hoping that someone will come through on what he promised. In prayer, you'll express the full range of human feeling and desire – directed towards God. Be careful of making prayer pietistic, as if it were a "religious" activity or "spiritual" feelings.

Instead of A.C.T.S., I like to use 1 Thessalonians 5:16-18. This guides my relationship with God using active verbs. **REJOICE ALWAYS**. Joy is the emotion of delight in a person, because of who that person is. **PRAY CONTINUALLY**. We ask for the help we need and want. This has two aspects. We need God's mercy for our sins and struggles. We need His aid amid life's hardships and pressures. **GIVE THANKS IN ALL CIRCUMSTANCES**. Thank you is how we respond to a gift, to what a person does that helps and blesses us. In a nutshell, these three aspects of prayer focus on who God is, what I need, and what God does. (If you look at it carefully, it covers the same ground as A.C.T.S., but comes out Adoration, then Confession & Supplication, and then Thanksgiving!) Those three verbs summarize all 150 Psalms, so 1 Thessalonians 5:16-18 operates like a hot link to the Psalms. There's where your life and what you are facing come alive in honest relationship with God.

LESSON TWO

BECOMING A CHILD
OF YOUR FATHER

*when Je tells the disciples they are
to be come like Je, he was saying they
should be like Him — Je is childlike
— he needs his father — can't do it an
his own*

I. INTRODUCTION: Becoming like a child is a central theme in Jesus' teaching and life.

1. *Unless you become like a little child you can't enter the kingdom of heaven." (Mark 10:13-16, Luke 18:15-17, Matt 19:13-15.) This would have been shocking to the disciples because children were not considered cute in the 1st century.*

2. *Associates humility of little children as model of kingdom behavior (Matt. 18:1-6; Mark 9:33-37; Luke 9:46-48).*

3. *Jesus refers to children's requests as models for kingdom praying (Luke 11:11-13, "Which of you fathers…" Matt. 7:7-11, "Which of you, if your son asks for…").*

4. *When the disciples report back to Jesus after their missionary trip that "even the demons submit to us in your name," Jesus burst forth, worshipping God that he has made the disciples like little children (Luke 10:17-21, also Matthew 11:25,26).*

5. *After the cleansing of the temple, the disabled and the little children pour in and begin worshipping Jesus. The Pharisees rebuke them, but Jesus praises them (Matthew 21:14-17).*

6. *Jesus is very childlike when he talks about his relationship with his heavenly Father. (John 5:19, "I do nothing on my own; I do just what I see my Father doing.")*

7. *Lord's Prayer is very childlike, using simple language. Possibly begin with "Abba."*

8. *"Abba, Father." At Gethsemane (Mark 14:36), Jesus addressed his Father by the very personal "Abba", the way a child would speak to his or her father. Most scholars feel that Jesus used "Abba" in addressing his heavenly Father. Jesus' usage made such an impression on the disciples that it was one of the few Aramaic words that cross over into the Greek speaking church. (Romans 8:15; Galatians 4:6).*

II. WHAT ARE LITTLE CHILDREN LIKE? HOW DO THEY ASK?

1. Children are not afraid to begin with themselves—their feelings, their problems, their lives.

- *Start from where you are when you go to pray.*
  - ~ *We get frozen by our selfishness. When we start praying we are confronted by our self-preoccupation and our wandering mind. We freeze, thinking, "Prayer isn't supposed to be like this. There must be something wrong with me." Then we give up in despair.*
  - ~ *But little children don't get frozen.*
  - ~ *Parents don't scold their little children for being self-absorbed or fearful.*
  - ~ *Illustration of Kim's first step. I can see it as clearly as if it happened three minutes ago. She took one step to her great-grandmother from my arms. We didn't say, "Oh Kim, that was good and all, but you know you are three now and about two years late on the whole thing."*

- *~ If you don't crawl, you won't walk.*
- Go to God as you are.
  - *~ If you don't, then what is really on your mind will come to the surface and feel like a distraction. Instead of fighting that distraction, go with it to God.*
  - *~ Matt. 11:28. Jesus doesn't say, "All you who are organized and can concentrate in prayer, come to me and I will give you rest." (More in Lesson 4.)*
- *Gospel: In the gospel you come as you are to God. Prayer is no different. If you try to fix yourself up, you kill the gospel, you kill prayer.*
- *Why so important?*
  - *~ You've got to be real in prayer and relationships.*
  - *~ "The real you has to meet the real God."*
  - *~ Hate saying this: "Got to be in touch with yourself."*
  - *~ Instead of being frozen by yourself, begin with yourself.*
  - *~ If you don't begin with yourself, that is where you'll end up.*
  - *~ By bringing yourself to God you'll end up being less self-centered!*
- *Often we don't even know if we are depressed, sad, anxious, or mean.*
  - *~ "What's bugging me?"*
  - *~ Go with your dyslexia.*
  - *~ Jesus accepts people where they are.*
  - *~ Accept where you are. Doesn't mean it's where you will be.*
  - *~ Example: Jesus with Nathaniel in John 1:46-47 Nathaniel: "Can anything good come out of Nazareth?" Jesus: "Behold an Israelite in whom there is not guile."*

2. Children learn a great deal by playing.

- *A child learns to play first. Learn the most basic things about life by playing.*

~ Illustration of Courtney compared with our dog, Riley, using the "Object Concept" from Piaget.
- *Go with your mind bouncing.*
  - *~ How to play: Take a passage of scripture that you enjoy and read it, think about it, talk it to God.*
  - *~ Caution: you won't be "doing" anything, just playing, that's okay.*
  - *~ Not concentrating, your mind flitting.*

3. Begin by Asking Like a Child.

Q. *What kinds of things do little children ask for? How often do they ask? What does "no" mean?*
- *Children ask for everything. They have no sense of limits.*
- *It doesn't get any better as teenagers. A "No" from their parent is just interesting information while they regroup and consider another angle.*
- *Illustration: our son John at seven months with his first word, "Bubba." We didn't say, "Not only are you pronouncing it wrong, but this is part of a selfish pattern in your life. John you are being too demanding."*
- *Little children begin by expecting their mom or dad to help.*

Maturity eventually develops a sense of limits, but first learn maturity by asking.

God will mature you. He will show you how to ask, but you've got to get into the race.

4. Speak Like a Child.

* Use natural language.
  Examples of Unnatural Language:
  ~ *King James language.*
  ~ *Passionate, deep, conversational language.*
* Language of prayer in the Bible is just normal speech.
  ~ Jesus teaching the Lord's Prayer: Matt 6:9-14.
  If this was the first time you heard the prayer, it is not immediately clear that prayer ends in verse 13.
  ~ Paul's Ephesians' prayer.
  Eph. 1:15-20 (hard to tell where prayer ends)
  Eph. 3:1 (starts, then interrupts himself)
  Eph. 3:14-20 (finally finishes his prayer)

* *Not clear where Paul begins and ends praying. He doesn't have any special prayer language.*

* *Ephesians 1-3 is a great example of ADD praying. Paul moves in and out of praying.*

 PRAYER ASSIGNMENT: Take five minutes now to be a little child with your Father: Begin with yourselves. Where you are? What are you thinking about? What is important to you now? (It might be wrong, but first, talk to God about it before you make a moral judgment. Not only do we make moral judgments about others too quickly but also we do the same thing with ourselves. So we cut off God from the gray areas of our lives.)

GROUP DISCUSSION

Q. What was it like to pray like a child?
Write their answers on the flip chart.

Final Reflections:

- *In that prayer time you were experiencing your Sonship.*

- *The spirit of Jesus was crying out in your heart, "Abba, Father." The spirit of prayer is the spirit of Sonship. The 3rd person of the Trinity lives in us and cries out. When we slow down and become like a little child, we make room for the Spirit. He prays like a child saying, "Abba." You are experiencing your Sonship.*

- *You stopped trying to be something you were not and let the Spirit speak through you.*

- *The immediate result of being led by the Spirit is freedom. Galatians 5:1, "It is for freedom that Christ has set you free."*

THE
LORD'S
PRAYER

"Our Father" is at the heart of the Lord's prayer and this lesson. If you learn to go as a child to your heavenly Father then everything else in prayer flows.

David Powlison's Reflections

One way of summarizing this lesson is that in prayer you are getting in touch with your circumstances, yourself, and your God. A real person in a real world with real struggles goes to a real God. I often don't even like to use the word "prayer," because it has artificial or dutiful overtones. The word takes on the flavor of religiosity or ritual, rather than simply meaning a direct conversation with someone who can help. In daily life, we use normal speech when we're glad to see someone, need their help on something, and feel grateful for help they've given. If you talked with your friends the way we often "pray" with God, they'd think you'd lost your mind!

For example, friends of mine are going through a hard situation with their daughter. When we talk together, our human conversation follows a pattern identical to the pattern of prayer.

1. "What are you facing?" Their circumstances are difficult. Their daughter is on a destructive path. The situation is confusing, with no obvious solution.
2. "What is this like for you?" They feel hurt. So much loss, disappointment, frustration, uncertainty about how to respond. They feel frightened, powerless, and angry at what is uncontrollable. We are people, not stones, so we feel keenly what happens to us.
3. "Who can help you? How will you respond constructively, and why?" They seek help, both from a friend and from God.

Normal human conversation brings together difficult circumstances, honest personal experience, and seeking help from someone you trust. That exactly mirrors what is going on as the Psalms grapple with troubles.

Prayer is realizing I can't do
life on my own
— I wasn't meant to
— John 5:19
— Je was the most dependent
person in the world
The worst thing for Je was to be
separated from the Father

LESSON THREE

BEGIN EARLY WITH YOUR FATHER

I. CHILDREN BEGIN EARLY

- *Illustration: If I know someone has little kids, I won't think twice about calling them on Saturday morning at 8:00. Usually they've been up for a couple of hours.*

- *Observations (not rules)*
  - ~ *Something about the morning time when you wake up that you're particularly open to talking to God. Most people who develop a rich prayer life begin in the morning. If you have to get coffee first, then do that.*
  - ~ *You can't pray in bed as your main prayer time. It's like trying to get good at a sport by just watching it. (You will pray even more in bed if you develop a main prayer time.)*
  - ~ *Some people do better praying while they walk.*

> *"Something about the morning, when you wake up that you're particularly open to talking to God."*

- Strong biblical pattern of getting up early to pray with God.
  - ~ Old Testament Pattern:
    Psalms: 5:3, 59:16, 88:13, 90:14, 92:1-2, 143:8
    Prophets: Isa. 50:4
  - ~ New Testament Pattern:
    Jesus in Luke 4:42, 5:16.
    See parallel passage in Mark 1:35. Jesus is going off to pray.

II. CHILDREN BEGIN WITH "BABY STEPS"

- Don't set impossible goals and then collapse so that you give up.
  - ~ *"I should be praying for half an hour. You have been a Christian for twenty years. You should know this stuff."*
  - ~ *Result: freezes us. "Something's really wrong with me."*
  - ~ *Set impossible standards and then collapse so you give up.*
  - ~ *Have a goal to pray for five minutes. Quickly moving to a position where you discover you've prayed overtime. You just got lost in praying, in being with God.*
- Take small pieces and then add to that.

III. CHILDREN PRAY OUT LOUD (NOT ON VIDEO)

- Jesus' personal pattern of praying (Hebrews 5:7) was to pray out loud. Going to a closet not only keeps you from showing off in prayer (Matthew 6:5,6), but it also allows you to pray out loud comfortably and avoid disturbing others.
- 95% of the Psalms have out loud cues such as *voice, cry,* or *shout.* So many prayer troubles arise from getting lost in one's head.
- Praying out loud is a way of making prayer concrete, of fighting the unbelief that permeates our world. I'm talking out loud to a real God who acts in my world.

Final Reflections:
- *If you pray more, you have less time to do things. Therefore, the very act of praying means there has to be more room for God to work.*
- *Principle: You do less when you pray more.*
- *How do you get up earlier to pray?*
- *What can you do in a half-hour?*

Four simple guidelines to starting a prayer life:
- Get out of bed.
- Get comfortable.
- Start with five minutes.
- Be consistent.

GROUP DISCUSSION
(Divide into small groups of 4-5 people if your group is larger than 12-15).

Q. If you decide to have a half hour prayer time in the morning, what practical steps will you need to take to make that happen?

Q. How long should I try to pray in the morning? (Don't set your goal too high. Consistency is more important than length.)

 PRAYER ASSIGNMENT (NOT ON VIDEO): Create a "prayer closet" (Matt. 6:5,6) by finding a place in the house/building to pray out loud comfortably. If you aren't used to doing this, you will feel a little awkward at first.

 The Lord's Prayer is a "baby step" prayer because it is short and simple. Anyone can pray it. Jesus models that by meeting with his Father early in the morning.

David Powlison's Reflections

Another way to approach "baby steps" is not to think about either time spent or getting through a list of requests. Instead, focus on two things. First, what is happening right now? What are you facing today, this moment? Second, what is one thing about God that is relevant? (Keep truth simple. For example, "I will never leave you or forsake you; I am with you" always applies every day.) Put these two things together and talk it out.

For example, is there something good that has just happened? Thank God now, because "You are good and do good" (Psalm 119:68). Or perhaps you are walking outside. Who made that cloud formation overhead? Worship him, because he created the heavens and the earth and everything in it. Do you feel plagued with guilt over something you did or said yesterday? Confess it aloud to God, naming your wrong, and thanking him that "there is forgiveness with you" (Psalm 130:4). Are you worrying ("obsessing") about something coming up later today? Cast your cares on him because he cares for you.

Focus on the existential or immediate quality of prayer, and it won't be dull or rote or clogged with pious phrases. Charles Spurgeon expressed it well: "It is not necessary in the closet to ask for every supposable good thing. Ask for what you now need, and, as a rule, keep to present needs. Ask for it plainly, as before God, who does not regard your fine expressions. You are before the Lord; let your words be few but let your heart be fervent" (*Effective Prayer*).

LESSON FOUR

HELPLESSNESS

The Key to Effective Praying

The concepts in this lesson are an expansion of Point 1 of Lesson 2.

I. WE CONSTRUCT A "HOLINESS CHART"
   (i.e., Create Artificial Spirituality)

STEP #1—Try to be Spiritual. Start out to get good at praying. A sense that "I need to do this."

STEP #2—Frustrated Trying to be Spiritual. We are confronted with our sinfulness.
Mind wanders, begin thinking about everything you have to do. Unique problem in prayer: brought face to face with your own selfishness as in no other area. Not sure how to go about doing prayer. Seems selfish to just ask.

STEP #3—"I'm not Spiritual." We stop praying. *Most of us stop doing what doesn't work. "Something's wrong with me." We're embarrassed. "Nothing happened." "I haven't gotten anything done." "Well, I'll pray during the day."*

STEP #4—Don't pray.

Fortunately: "Don't pray" works because no one notices when you don't pray. Satan wins.
- *You have unique problems (you do).*
- *You are only concerned about yourself (you are).*
- *Nothing is happening (you are correct).*
- *Gets us all tied up in knots.*

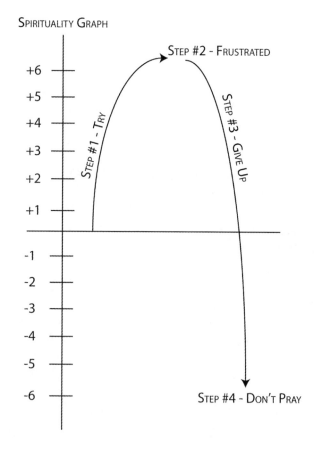

SPIRITUALITY GRAPH

STEP #2 - FRUSTRATED

STEP #1 - TRY

STEP #3 - GIVE UP

+6
+5
+4
+3
+2
+1
-1
-2
-3
-4
-5
-6

STEP #4 - DON'T PRAY

II. REALIZE YOU NEED HELP

Jesus says in Matthew 11:28:
(*This point is first introduced in Lesson 2 (Point 1) and expanded on here.*)

> MATT. 11:28 "COME TO ME, ALL YOU WHO ARE WEARY AND HEAVY-LADEN AND I WILL GIVE YOU REST."

Jesus doesn't say:

> *"Come to me, all you whose minds have stopped wandering and aren't worrying and I will give you rest."*

> *"Come to me all you who have learned how to pray and concentrate in prayer?"*

What would be the point of coming if our hearts are already at rest?

III. OUR HELPLESSNESS POINTS US TO THE GOSPEL

* Gospel doesn't work if you think you have it all together; it only works when you know you are messed up.
* Prayer is a mirror of the Gospel.
* "We look at the inadequacy of our praying and give up thinking something is wrong with us—God looks at the adequacy of his Son and delights in our sloppy praying."
* *Restlessness is the normal condition of our disabled hearts. To try to get rid of restlessness before you pray or as you pray is like trying to save yourself. Point of lesson is to be honest about your real needs.*

- Gospel and Prayer
  - ~ The Gospel: The Father takes you as you are because of Jesus and gives you his gift of salvation.
  - ~ Prayer: You go to the Father as you are and the Father gives you his gift of friendship and help.
- Romans 8:32: If God gave you His only Son isn't He going to do everything else in your life that you need?

IV. GO TO GOD AS YOU ARE

More mature Christians are…
  - ~ More desperate so they come more quickly.
  - ~ More aware of their limitations, so they feel the need for more prayer.

V. OUR WEAKNESSES ARE ALWAYS A SURPRISE TO US

- We stay in Christian fatalism.
  - ~ *We try to get away from the tension, solve the problem instead of realizing we can take the tension to God.*
- Jesus: "weakness is the condition of your soul where I am most available."
  - ~ *I frequently don't pray about my worries.*
  - ~ *Usually I am a good way into a worry before I even realize that I've been worrying.*
- Whole point of prayer is you go to God with things that aren't figured out.
- "Come As I Am": *God doesn't want us to come perfected.*

VI. THE BOOK OF JOHN:
A STUDY IN HELPLESSNESS

- John 2:3—no wine; 4:5—no water; 4:47—no health; 5:7—no help; 6:5—no bread; 9:1—no sight; 11—no life
- Prayer is taking your helplessness to Jesus.
  - ~ *My Sense: I should be praying right. I shouldn't be worrying. I should have it together. You are just going to Jesus with the state of your heart (it's a mess...that's the point).*
  - ~ *O. Hallesby: "The condition necessary to prayer is helplessness."*
  - ~ *Prayer is helplessness.*
  - ~ *Prayer is taking your helplessness to Jesus.*

VII. THE HEART OF ALL GOOD PRAYER:
I NEED JESUS

- *Story of our camping trip in summer of '90. "I need Jesus."*
- *Learning to pray for my family.*
  - ~ *My words to them are limited.*
  - ~ *My words to God for them are very powerful.*
- *Jesus isn't asking us to do anything that he isn't doing.*

  > JN: 5:19, 30: "I DO NOTHING ON MY OWN. I DO JUST WHAT I SEE MY FATHER DOING."

  - ~ *Kids in wheelchairs at speaking computer camp. (O. Hallesby talks about kids in wheel chairs. How humbling it is to have to ask for everything. Helplessness has become a part of who they are as people. Therefore grateful for the least help you give them.)*
  - ~ *Are you asking me to become incompetent? No, just to realize that you are! That is what poverty of spirit is.*

WE THINK: Strong Christians pray a lot. If I were a stronger Christian, I'd pray more.
TRUTH: Only when we are weak do we pray. A strong Christian is just more aware of his/her weaknesses. Prayer is just bringing your weaknesses to God.

 PRAYER ASSIGNMENT: Reflect on areas in your life where you are helpless.

Paul's Prayer in Eph. 3

> EPH. 3:14-21 "For this reason I kneel before the Father, from whom his whole family in heaven and on earth derives its name. I pray that out of his glorious riches he may strengthen you with power through his Spirit in your inner being, so that Christ may dwell in your hearts through faith. And I pray that you, being rooted and established in love, may have power, together with all the saints, to grasp how wide and long and high and deep is the love of Christ, and to know this love that surpasses knowledge—that you may be filled to the measure of all the fullness of God. Now to him who is able to do immeasurably more than all we ask or imagine, according to his power that is at work within us, to him be glory in the church and in Christ Jesus throughout all generations, for ever and ever! Amen."

THE LORD'S PRAYER

The Lord's Prayer involves a radical de-centering of ourselves by first focusing on God and his kingdom. But our personal "kingdoms" are so strong that we must begin with grace, with the welcoming Father, just as the Lord's Prayer begins with "our Father." This is specifically mentioned in the Lord's Prayer when we forgive as we have been forgiven. At the heart of kingdom obedience is the cry, "I need Jesus."

David Powlison's Reflections

Paul Miller's father, Jack Miller, was my pastor for many years. One of the profoundly simple things I learned from Jack came from his understanding of the first beatitude, "Blessed are the poor in spirit, for theirs is the kingdom of heaven" (Matt. 5:3). He said that the first beatitude was not "first" in the sense that you figure it out and move on to the next one. It's not like first base in baseball, a way station on your way to second, third, and home. Instead, the first beatitude is first in the same way that the foundation of a multi-story building comes first. It always undergirds the whole building. It establishes the shape of the entire structure. The foundation has omnipresent effects. "Poor in spirit" simply means a deep inner sense of need for help from outside yourself. A beggar has no money, food, health, safety, bank account, resumé, or marketable skills. Someone else must provide and protect. And so it is with us. When I know I need what only God can give, then I pray straight-on, honest prayers.

LESSON FIVE

ASK YOUR FATHER ANYTHING

I. THE DYNAMIC OF PRAYER: THE INFINITE-PERSONAL GOD

- Infinite God is also personal
  - ~ *Ancient World always struggled between the Universal vs. Particular.*
  - ~ *Eastern Religion: Universal.*
  - ~ *Western/Greek: Particular.*

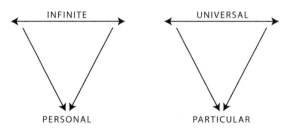

- God of Heavens dwelt in the Temple
  - ~ *Scandal of Jewish monotheism that the God of Israel claimed to be the one God of the whole earth vs. local deity of ancient world.*

~ *I Kings 20:28: Man of God came to King of Israel and told him, "The Arameans think that the Lord is the god of the hills and not a god of the valleys." They assume the Lord is just a local deity. Big mistake.*

~ *Jews didn't worship emperor. Seemed odd to Romans, "He's just our local deity."*

~ *N.T. Wright: Why so many Messiahs in 1st century. They believed that God would act in history.*

~ *Hindu became a Christian after reading Matthew 1. Attracted to particularity of it.*

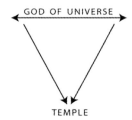

- Infinite God in the Person of Jesus:
  ~ *Isa. 57:15: God dwells in the heavens and with Me!*
  ~ *Psalm 23 is startling to the ancient mind. God's personal attention to me is unheard of.*
  ~ *This is the idea of the incarnation.*

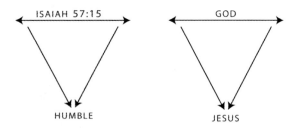

- God of universe is concerned about me.
  - ~ *In this context, prayer makes perfect sense.*
  - ~ *Prayer is a repeating moment of incarnation.*
  - ~ *Explains both the awesomeness of prayer and why it is so daunting to us. (Implicit in many of our comments from lesson 1, "Why is Prayer Hard?")*
  - ~ *It is an error to think prayer is just relationship. Example of book on Prayer that minimizes God's activity: The author said, "Look at all the prayers that Christian women offered for their sick children that God didn't answer." NO. God intersects history. Constantly.*

  > "The problems we have in prayer are all connected to believing whether the infinite God dwells within me."

  - ~ *We draw an invisible line between us and God. Line is from the fall. Our desire to draw the line is from the fall.*
  - ~ *Kant: Division between science (what is real, what we know for sure) and spirituality (what we believe, religious truth). God is only on the top but he never messes with the lower story. No. My God is alive. He's not in a closet.*
  - ~ *Not caught in the Greek's cycle.*

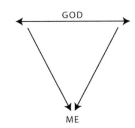

II. "ASK ANYTHING AND I WILL DO IT"
- Jesus at the Last Supper

> JOHN 14:12-14: I TELL YOU THE TRUTH,
> ANYONE WHO HAS FAITH IN ME WILL DO WHAT I
> HAVE BEEN DOING. HE WILL DO EVEN GREATER
> THINGS THAN THESE, BECAUSE I AM GOING TO
> THE FATHER. AND I WILL DO WHATEVER YOU
> ASK IN MY NAME, SO THAT THE SON MAY BRING
> GLORY TO THE FATHER. YOU MAY ASK ME FOR
> ANYTHING IN MY NAME, AND I WILL DO IT.

The Infinite will work in your life.
John 15:7; 15:16, 16:23
Summary: 6 times in these verses you see "ask anything" or "whatever you ask."

 Q. Why does "Ask anything and I will do it" make us nervous?
~ like a cup with a fire hose.
~ maybe God is a tribal deity.

CHICAGO
~ It is not our experience.
~ Makes God into a Santa Claus.
~ I should only be asking for spiritual things.
~ I ask and it doesn't come.
~ Puts me in a humble position, vulnerable.
~ I'd lose control. Involves a leap of faith.
~ Is he exaggerating?
~ Watch out for what you ask for, you might get it.
~ God does it on his timetable.

PHILADELPHIA
~ We've prayed and it didn't happen the way we asked.
~ Can I really do this?
~ Failure. I don't like to fail. If I pray and it doesn't work

then is my faith real? What is wrong with me? What is wrong with God?

~ Will we really do greater things than Jesus?

~ Fearful of how God will answer.

III. COMMENTARY ON JOHN 14:13-14: (YOU AREN'T THE ONLY ONES WHO ARE NERVOUS.)

"A cursory reading of John 14:13-14 may give people the indication that Jesus will give a person anything he wants, so long as he asks for it "in Jesus' name".... Satan would love to get us to believe the lie that God answers our prayers according to our will. His hope is that once we discover that God is not answering our requests for riches, fame, and glory...we chalk Christianity up to being a sham and accuse Jesus of breaking his promises....

"...Jesus is really saying, "Ask me to do anything for you in the area of my work and I will do it." ... Now how do we know that this is the correct understanding from the context?

~ "The significance of the name of Jesus is one indication...the very name of Jesus points to his work of redemption.

~ "The significance of the will of the Father is another indication. This work of redemption, Jesus says a few short verses ago, is the Father's will; 'it is the Father, living in me, who is doing this work' (v. 10)... It is the work of ministry that Jesus has been doing that He is interested in completing through the church.

~ "The goal of glorifying the Father is a third indication.... The 'whatever' of verse 13 and the 'anything' of verse 14 refers specifically to the work Christ has done through the church that will glorify the Father... What we have in these two passages is a means by which Jesus completes His work of ministry through the church on earth. If we intend to be effective witnesses, we must employ God's assistance through prayer, asking only that His will be done, not ours. Only then do we have answered prayer."

- *Paul's response to this commentary:*
  - ~ *Agree: prayer is not magic.*
    - ▫ *Classic example: Israelites taking the ark into battle in I Sam. 4.*
    - ▫ *Prayer is not us getting power over God to do our will. Some Christians talk this way.*
    - ▫ *God is not a genie where we can use him to achieve our will divorced from a relationship of fellowship and submission to him.*
  - ~ *Disagree: His analysis, by a thousand qualifications, kills the impact of what Jesus says.*
    - ▫ *Even though Jesus says "whatever" or "anything" five times, he says that Jesus really doesn't mean "whatever." Makes me nervous doing that with Scripture.*
    - ▫ *Is he protecting God from looking like a failure?*
    - ▫ *His whole emphasis is on what God can't do.*
  - ~ *Defines it as only applying to Jesus' work of redemption.*
    - ▫ *True, because Jesus' work touches every part of my life.*
    - ▫ *But he implies that work of redemption only applies when you are witnessing.*
    - ▫ *Can't I also feel my Father's pleasure when I am taking out the trash?*
    - ▫ *In his earthly life Jesus was concerned with the physical as well as the spiritual.*
    - ▫ *I sense a sacred/secular dichotomy. I think we do that in our lives.*
    - ▫ *Illustration of businessman working on a project, "I haven't prayed about it. It seemed selfish."*

IV. JESUS WANTS US TO ENGAGE HIM

- Two Dangers (James 4:2-3)
  - ~ Not Asking.
    You don't ask. You live your life on your own. You don't bring your needs to God. You don't let him intersect with your life.
  - ~ Asking Wrongly.
    When you do ask, you ask for a serpent instead of bread. Your heavenly Father loves you too much to give you a viper.

Q. *What is the most dangerous cliff for you?*
  - *Most Christians don't think their way through the day through prayer.*
  - *Imagine you have a very wealthy friend who enjoys giving money away, who enjoys you telling him your needs. Quirk: he wants to be your friend. He wants you to get to know him.*

Q. *Of these two dangers which one is Jesus most concerned about in John 14-16?*
  - *Jesus' heavy emphasis on encouraging us to ask implies that his concern is that we don't ask.*

NOT ASKING

Separated from God

ASK SELFISHLY

Prayer as magic
(getting God to do my will)

GOOD ASKING

GOD	GOD	ME
ME	↑ ME	↓ GOD

ANTIDOTE:
ASK BOLDLY
*"Abba, Father, everything is
possible for you...take this
cup from me..."*

ANTIDOTE:
SURRENDER COMPLETELY
*"...Yet not what I will,
but what you will..."*

V.   YES, THERE ARE TWO QUALIFICATIONS:

- FIRST: Abiding. John 15:7: "If you remain in me and my words remain in you…." But Jesus' main emphasis is our asking and his promise, not on the qualifiers.
  - ~ *Absolutely central. In verses 15:1-6, Jesus says you can't do anything outside of me.*
  - ~ *You don't wait until you are abiding and then ask. You ask in the process of learning how to abide.*
  - ~ *7 and 16 are like the top layers of the sandwich; "in me you can do anything," (15:7-16 is a chiasm).*
  - ~ *Center is joy. Inner layers are obedience.*

- SECOND: Praying in the name of Jesus.
  - ~ *Praying in Jesus' name means that when I sat down to pray for my daughter this morning my mind wandered. I probably didn't even ask for just the right thing. Maybe I only got out a couple of incoherent sentences. But because I prayed in Jesus' name, my prayer had a royal authority to it. It bore the very stamp of Jesus in it.*
  - ~ *My prayer is like a poorly dressed beggar standing outside the palace of the great king stammering out a halting message that is barely intelligible. But I come in the name of Jesus. When I whisper his name, the guards snap to attention, the door flies open, and I am ushered down the long hallway into the throne room of the great king.*
  - ~ *The name of Jesus means that Jesus transforms my prayers into spiritual language. Jesus isn't just the Savior of my soul; he's also the Savior of my prayers. They come before the throne of God as the prayers of Jesus.*
  - ~ *His seal on the package not only guarantees that the package gets through but it transforms the package. Rom 8:26, 27, "In the same way, the Spirit helps us in our weaknesses. We do not know what we ought to pray for, but the Spirit himself intercedes for us with groans that words cannot express. And he who searches our hearts knows the mind of the Spirit, because the Spirit intercedes for the saints in accordance with God's will."*

Q. *If you are going to take Jesus at his word ("Ask the Father for whatever you want in my name and I will do it for you"), what is the first thing you have to ask yourself? "What do I want?"*

Q. What is difficult about the question, "What do I want?"
- *Do we really know what we want?*
- *This is where abiding comes in. The very process of asking leads you into abiding.*

Thomas Merton, "Why do we spend our lives striving to be something that we would never want to be, if we only knew what we wanted? Why do we waste our time doing things which...are just the opposite of what we were made for?"

> *The closer we get to the heart of God, the more we begin to want what God wants.*

Q. *Honestly, isn't money one of the first things that we'd ask for if we could get anything we would want?*

Q. *What would happen to your life if you got $5,000,000? (Makes you distant from people. People start coming after you for giving, etc. You thought you were asking for bread when in fact you were asking for a stone.)*

 Q. What are categories that we tend not to pray for?
- *Mundane things (too unimportant).*
- *Personal things (too selfish).*
- *Change in others (too controlling).*
- *Emotional change in me: "Would you give me more joy?" (too unusual).*
- *Change in me. Means admitting to myself that I have the problem: "Lord this morning I have a mean spirit. Until it goes away would you help me keep my mouth shut?" (too humble).*
- *Things we are good at (too easy...we don't need help).*
- *Material things (too selfish...which it might be, but if it is, God will shape that).*
- *Overwhelming impossible needs (too impossible).*
- *Learning to Pray for my family:*

- *Husbands: "My wife bristles when I ask her to help me. Help her not to be afraid of submission."*
- *Wives: "My husband is withdrawn, and it is driving me crazy."*
- *I find a simple Scripture passage that describes how I'd like this person to be acting and pray for that person using that Scripture.*
- *Each engagement with God, each prayer request becomes a fascinating story. The infinite becomes personal.*
  - *I see my heart, my grumpiness.*
  - *I see God do things in them that I had nothing to do with.*
  - *Example: How can I get Kim up in the morning so she isn't grumpy?*
  - *Example: How can I get more of God's Word into the life of one of my kids? Led me to teaching the youth group at church. Humbling. Hard.*
  - *Prayer becomes a primary way of parenting.*
  - *The infinite is concerned with my family.*
- *Christianity is a physical religion. We believe in a good creation.*

Examples from the Disciples:
- A Mundane Request: Mark 8:14-21—the disciples forget to bring bread.
- A Personal Request: Mark 10:13-16—not important enough to interrupt Jesus.

Don't be afraid to ask. God will shape you in your asking. You learn to abide by asking and dialoguing with your Father.

PRAYER ASSIGNMENT: Make a list of things that you tend not to pray about. Be honest with God. He will shape you. Put your real wants out there.

And/or write out some of the things you'd like to see changed in your spouse, child, parent, friend, or co-worker and find Scripture for them.

 The more we ask God, the more our desires are in tune with him. Christ begins to rule in the lives of my children, my spouse, and my life as I ask God to do what I can't do. I can't change my spouse. I can't make the kingdom come in my family. But God can.

David Powlison's Reflections

The generosity of our heavenly and his desire to give us good gifts is reflected in the simplest reading of the request for daily bread in The Lord's Prayer. In the Greek it literally says, "Give us tomorrow's bread today." Not just today's bread but tomorrow's as well. God's normal blessings include a measure of predictability to life, also to be trusted by dependent faith (see Deuteronomy 8 for how faith is tested in both the radical and the normal). An agricultural society usually stores up most foods an entire year at a time. Crops are as much God's provision as manna. Your paycheck and retirement savings are gifts from his hand.

So we ask our Father for food and for healing, for protection in travels and for good weather, for calm wisdom when taking a test in school and…. We are ultimately asking that he would show himself on the stage of history, even in these "small" things.

LESSON SIX

ENTERING YOUR FATHER'S STORY THROUGH PRAYER

Key Issue: Why doesn't God answer my prayers?

I. STORY OF ISRAEL
- Temple is destroyed.
- Jerusalem is destroyed.
- Walls are down.
- Kingdom is gone.
- King is gone.
- Kingship is gone.
- Deported.
- Unbelievers brought in.
- Glory has departed from Israel.

Israel was in agony: Psalm 137:1, "By the rivers of Babylon we sat and wept when we remembered Zion."

Return from captivity only made it worse. Haggai said to Zerubbabel, "Who of you who is left saw the house in its former glory? How does it look to you now? Does it not seem to you as nothing?" (2:3)

Hope: "In a little while I will once more shake the heavens and the earth, the sea and the dry land. I will shake all the nations, and the desired of the nations will come, and I will fill this house with glory…the glory of this present house will be greater than the glory of the former house" (2:7, 9).

Precisely why there were so many 1st century would-be Messiahs. The Jews believed that (1) their situation was unnatural and that (2) God would act on their behalf (3) in history. (cf N.T. Wright. He points out that critical scholars are just not in touch with the first century data when they have a Jewish community creating a 'spiritual' Jesus that has nothing to do with reality. They just didn't think in transcendental categories.)

II. HOPE/REALITY CHART

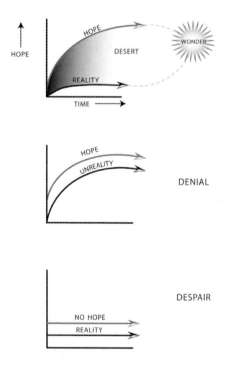

- *What does the tension between hope and reality feel like?*
  - *~ It hurts.*
  - *~ You aren't in control.*
  - *~ God's word doesn't equal the situation.*
  - *~ Promise of God almost makes it worse.*
  - *~ Hope is more painful than despair.*
  - *~ Abraham: Romans 4:18-21.*
- *Temptation to Denial (Pentecostal Tendency, James, "You ask wrongly.").*
  - *~ No look at reality, no painful waiting.*
  - *~ But ultimately despair.*
- *Temptation to Run (Presbyterian Tendency, James, "You don't ask."*
  - *~ No hope, no pain.*
  - *~ But no miracle. No intervention of God.*
  - *~ Ahaz,: (Is 7:10-14).*

Our daughter Kim

- *Jill was pregnant with Kim when she claimed the promise from Ps. 121, "No harm will befall you."*
- *God gave us a harmed child: Bright and cheerful but brain damaged. Poor fine motor skills, can't speak or write.*
- *Hurt to hope. Jill was in agony. Easier not to expect something better.*
- *Ashley, our second daughter, struggling with God's existence at age 14. She'd lost her contact while camping on the ground on the forest floor filled with leaves. "Ashley, let's pray." "What good does it do? God doesn't answer our prayer for Kim."*
- *Something that affects our family every day.*
- *"What's it like?" Like a death sentence.*
- *"Why don't you just give Kim to God? I do every day."*

III. PERMANENT WEAKNESS: SUFFERING IN PRAYER

- *Gap = Suffering is the quickest way to learn how to pray.*
- *Suffering puts you face to face with your inability, your weakness, and your lack of control.*
- *Completely boxed in, you are able to rebuild the ancient and rusty prayer machine because it is the only thing you have.*
- *Biblical metaphor: Desert.*
  - ~ *A desert is a place with no life in it. Nothing to sustain you.*
  - ~ *Everyone that God uses he takes through a desert: Abraham, Jacob, Joseph, Moses, David, Jesus, Paul.*
  - ~ *You learn to pray in the desert. The desert is the place where God takes his people to learn to pray.*
  - ~ *A desert is a place of pain…maybe a relationship, a job, a child, or an illness that you can't control or eliminate from your life. These deserts are the windows to the heart of God.*
  - ~ *When you are in a desert, you learn what your real thirsts are: Psalm 63:1, "O God, you are my God, earnestly I seek you; my soul thirsts for you, my body longs for you, in a dry and weary land where there is no water."*
  - ~ *You come face to face with the powerlessness of your idols.*
  - ~ *Idols die for lack of food in the desert.*
  - ~ *Story of Paul and Jill with Kim. God's gift to humble two proud people.*

IV. WHY DOES GOD WAIT?

- *We are focused on the situation. God is focused on us.*
  - ~ *We come to the end of ourselves. We lose control.*
  - ~ *Learn to pray.*
- *God is also focused on the situation.*
  - ~ *Not merely interested in change in you. A tendency to over-spiritualize suffering.*

- ~ *Prayer is relational (Learning to relate to God) and about asking (Learning to ask God to do things.).*
- ~ *He is writing a story. Watch for his hand, watch for story patterns.*
- ~ *You learn to know him in the story.*
- ~ *Overwhelming temptation is to drop out of the story.*
- *Jn. 15:7 "abiding" is what story is all about.*
  - ~ *Begin to see that what you thought was a serpent is really a loaf of bread. You didn't have the eyes to see it.*
- *Watching for Story.*
  - ~ *Our individual prayers function in terms of the whole pattern of God's activity.*
  - ~ *Need to write down the prayers so you don't lose the threads of the story.*
- *Relationship with a Spirit.*
- *Suffering changes your paradigm of this world.*
  - ~ *It lets you see the unseen.*
  - ~ *It makes the seen less valuable, important.*
  - ~ *In that context, prayer flows naturally.*

V. ISRAEL: SO WHAT WAS GOD DOING?

- *Temple.*
  - ~ *Imagine the simple prayer of an elderly Jewish peasant in 400 B. C., "God it hurts to look at this temple. Would you restore the temple so that it is as great as Solomon's temple?"*
  - ~ *What did God do? His answer is unbelievable. It is far more gigantic than the prayers. He sent his son to be the temple.*
- *King.*
  - ~ *An eternal king.*
  - ~ *An eternal kingdom.*

- *Local Church.*
  - ~ *God used the destruction of the temple and the removal of the Israelites to Babylon to create the synagogue structure, a kind of proto-local church. If temple worship had continued uninterrupted, we'd not had a model for the local church. The idea of "local church" was born in seed form.*
- *Bible.*
  - ~ *The Old Testament was born. Most scholars believed that the O.T. scrolls were organized during this time. That gave the early church the category of "Scripture" that, in turn, created the N.T.*
- *Theology.*
  - ~ *Purified Israel of Idolatry. Israel would never again worship other pagan gods.*
  - ~ *Monotheism became permanently central in Israel. This was the foundation of the Judeo-Christian thought, central to Western Civilization.*
- *Holiness.*
  - ~ *Purified Israel of inter-mixing with other nations.*
- *Missions.*
  - ~ *Dispersia became the framework for the early missionary movements of the church.*
- *Preparing for the Death of His Son.*
  - ~ *Their monotheism led them to kill Jesus for his claim to be God's son.*
  - ~ *Jesus' claim to authority over the temple was a key piece in their denunciation of him at the trial.*
  - ~ *Jesus desire to reach out to the unclean revolted them.*
  - ~ *They replaced idolatry of Baal with idolatry of the people of Israel.*
  - ~ *Their demand for a human king was rejected by Jesus but they read their own lusts into Jesus and accused him of that before Pilate.*

VI. PERSONAL STORY KIM (CONT'D FROM PAGE 49)

- *When Ashley lost her contacts, I prayed again. We bent down and there it was.*
- *She put our house under tremendous pressure.*
  - ~ *Illustration of Kim's effect on our house. It snowed and schools had a two hour delay. She freaked out because it messed up her schedule. Whining, crying, just driving all of us nuts. "Kim you are the only kid in Souderton School District who is upset that they missed the bus this morning!"*
  - ~ *Stop caring about secondary things. It burns out of you a desire to control when you have a child who you can't control.*
  - ~ *Illustration of Kim at a buffet dinner. She marched in, grabbed some lunch meat off a platter and sat down and ate it. Someone gave Jill a dirty look. We're a little slow to write that book on "How to Parent the Perfect Child." You are humbled by your inability to make something happen.*
- *The pressure that Kim brought into our home pushed me to realize that what I knew about love and the gospel was not adequate. It just wasn't working. It drove me into studying about Jesus.*
- *Explain Threads to this story:*
  - ~ *Kim's birth—Hunger for God. This world got gray— start of WHM in 1982.*
  - ~ *Pressure on Jill—"Do you love me?"—Beginning to learn to love—Falling in love with Jesus—Start of seeJesus.net in 1999.*
  - ~ *Humbling of our family.*
- *17 years later, we had forgotten about Jill's Psalm 121 prayers, I was doing a Bible study for our small group on Psalm 121, and I said to Jill, "Look, it has happened. Through Kim, God has saved our family from harm."*

- *God is also concerned for Kim. The universal is concerned for the particular. The infinite God is also personal. DO NOT OVERSPIRITUALIZE PRAYER. (Draw dotted line through middle of Personal/Infinite chart).*
  - ~ *Deaf school.*
  - ~ *Speaking computer.*
  - ~ *New method of Kim learning to speak.*
  - ~ *Those in turn have transformed Jill even more.*

VII. IDEA OF STORY AND JOURNAL WRITING

- *First autobiography that looked at the unconscious was Augustine's Confessions. When you encounter God, then you can really see yourself.*
- *The Puritan's picked up this style of reflective writing to discern the condition of their souls. It was one small step from seeing the interior of their hearts to the 19th century novel.*
- *In writing out our prayers we stand in that long tradition. Because God is the infinite-personal God, he is intimately involved with the details of my life. My prayers interact with this God-who-is-there giving meaning, purpose, and hope to my life. So writing out my prayers not only becomes a way of interacting with God, but a way of recording and reflecting on this life-full-of-meaning!*
- *For an example of journal writing look at the front page of this manual. You can see that I'm laying questions before God.*
- *To understand the answers, you need to be in touch with and understand the larger story of your life. Writing out your prayers in prayer journals helps you to do that.*

Q. *What is the difference between "no story" and "story"?*

NO STORY	STORY
BITTER	WAITING
ANGRY	WATCHING
AIMLESS	WONDERING
CYNICAL	PRAYING
	SUBMITTING

 PRAYER ASSIGNMENT: Using your journals, write a prayer to God or even better, just write to God. If you are not journaling this will be the beginning of you reflecting on your story.

 The Lord's Prayer is an invitation to enter into God's story for our lives, to become God-centered and put his rule plus his will at the center. It climaxes with a prayer to deliver us from evil. By becoming aware of the pattern of God's working through evil we can escape the twin dangers of denial and despair and see the rich pattern of God's grace in our lives.

David Powlison's Reflections

Most Christians think of their "testimony" in two ways. First, "my testimony" is the dark story that led up to becoming a Christian. When you "give your testimony," you stop after the moment of decision. Second, "my testimony" is the good person I've become since I became a Christian. If you "ruin your testimony," it means you sinned in some way that other people found out about. Now it's true that we bear witness to our Lord both by telling how he found us and by living a visibly changed life. But both of these tell only part of the whole story our testimony is to tell.

You bear witness to your Lord by the ongoing story of your need for the Lord's mercies. That includes the ways he sustains you in all your troubles: "Call on me in the day of trouble; I will rescue you, and you will honor me" (Psalm 50:15). It includes the many ways he picks you up after you fall: "If we confess our sins, he is faithful and just to forgive us and cleanse us from all unrighteousness" (1 Jo. 1:9). Your testimony is a story about the ongoing hand of the Lord in your life. And that is a reality that makes you pray much more realistically.

LESSON SEVEN

LEARNING TO LISTEN TO YOUR FATHER

I. CHILDREN BEGIN BY LISTENING, ABSORBING.

Learning to use a spiritual "ear" that we didn't know we had.
Kids learn their language by listening.

II. LISTENING TO GOD IN PRAYER

- Example of praying for my goals for a year.
  - ~ *"What should my goals be?...a complete blank."*
  - ~ *"Don't worry about goals. I'm going to work on your character this year."*
  - ~ *"What do I need to work on?"*
  - ~ *Thought came to me: "obvious, you know." I wrote down a list of seven things that God was convicting me about.*
- Example of hiring an assistant.
  - ~ *"The Person is under your nose."*
  - ~ *Turkey burger...I remembered.*

- Example of Bob Allums: "Not too long ago, I was inclined to pray for a certain woman. It was a heavy urge to pray for her and it lasted a few days. Finally, after much praying, I called her on the phone and told her that I sensed the Holy Spirit leading me to pray specifically for her in a Romans 8 kind of way. She was appreciative but I could tell she thought it a little on the "goofy" side. I fully understand that; you can't share that kind of thought with just anyone; they just wouldn't understand. I asked her if anything was "going on" in her life that would prompt such leadings of the Spirit. She said "no, not really." Well, this week, she called me to say that her husband said he didn't love her anymore. One of those "I love you but I'm not in love with you" kind of comments. It turns out that he was having an affair. I learned when I sense the need to pray for someone, I'm not going to question it; I'm just going to "do" it. In other words, if the Spirit leads us to intercede and we don't know why, it is all part of the story."

In prayer you are connecting with a personal, spiritual being.

III. TO WHAT DOES GOD DIRECT US?

- Wisdom (that thinks and acts as Jesus thinks and acts).
- Love (that treats people the way Jesus treats people).
- Repentance (that turns to God from 10,000 distractions).
- More Prayer (i.e., faith that continues to trust and relate to God).

CAUTIONS:
Must be tested by...
~ The authority of the Word.
~ The authority of the church.

IV. GOD SPEAKS THROUGH HIS WORD

- Something very mysterious about God's Word in prayer.
  - ~ *When you use a passage of Scripture such as Psalm 23 to pray with, prayer comes alive.*
  - ~ *"God I need you to be my shepherd today."*
  - ~ *"How are you preparing a table before me in the presence of my enemies?"*
  - ~ *"What does it mean that I will return to the temple of God?"*

- Danger: The Spirit without the Word.
  - ~ *Illustration: I would pray in the morning in our daughter Emily's room after she'd gotten up. Jill would go to the attic. "Paul, this is the voice of God speaking. Listen to your wife, she needs a new kitchen."*
  - ~ *Problem: the World, the Flesh, the Devil, and the Holy Spirit all come in on the same channel.*

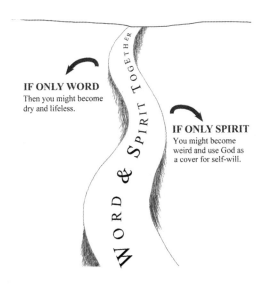

IF ONLY WORD
Then you might become dry and lifeless.

IF ONLY SPIRIT
You might become weird and use God as a cover for self-will.

WORD & SPIRIT TOGETHER

V. "CONSTANT IN PRAYER."

* *You'll wake up at night and discover you are singing. What's happening? Gal. 4:6, "Because you are sons, God sent the Spirit of his Son into our hearts, the Spirit who calls out Abba, Father." Jesus by the Spirit is in you praying to the Father.*
* "Constant in Prayer": One of Paul's favorite phrases. Notice how many times Paul links "always" or "constantly" with prayer (Rom. 1:9, 12:12; Eph. 1:16, 6:18; Col. 1:9, 4:2,12, I Thess. 1:2, 2:13, 3:10, 5:17; II Thess. 1:11; II Tim. 1:3).
* *Must shut down the "Kingdom of Noise" (C. S. Lewis).*
* *Like an open modem. You are in the car and it's like you are live to heaven. And you'll think, "What do I want? Where am I? Who needs help and protection?"*
* *You'll discover your heart bending towards God with simple phrases, maybe just saying Jesus' name over and over again the way a little child will a nursery rhyme.*
* *The more you pray, the more you pray.*

> *"The more you listen, the more God speaks. The more you pray ...the more you pray.*

 PRAYER ASSIGNMENT: Take Psalm 23 and begin to pray through it. Turn it into a prayer. Be quiet before God as you pray. Let God personalize his Word to your heart and your needs. Let him speak to you.

See Appendix B for an essay on "God's Speaking" written by Paul Miller.

See Appendix C for a brief explanation of "Divine Reading" or praying Scripture to God.

The Lord's Prayer

We listen to God so he can be the center of our life. If our listening to God is not shaped by God's Word, then we are really saying, "My kingdom come." We try to use prayer to make our will happen. When we are constant in prayer, then we are constantly crying out to God for his leading.

David Powlison's Reflections

The Holy Spirit's personal, on-the-fly leading is always into the revealed will of God. So when I ask for greater wisdom, it should not surprise me when he actually helps me to see the world through different eyes and to respond in a creative, constructive way. Such changes are produced not simply because I've rationalistically restructured my thought process and implemented my plans and resolve to act a certain way. That would be a sort of deism, as if God leaves us to our own devices and abilities. But neither is such wisdom simply some odd, wildcard impulse that overrides both Scripture and my conscious thoughts and intentions. That would be a sort of God-of-the-gaps, as if God's hand is only discerned in extraordinary, inexplicable events. The real God works in the normal affairs of his world. The real God works in the normal affairs of our lives.

We need wisdom. He gives wisdom without reproaching us for our need. It's not an abstract attribute of WISDOM; it's situation-specific wisdom. We need to love. When we find ourselves caring for a particular person, bearing someone else's welfare on our hearts, the Spirit is working his fruit of patience, kindness, and concern. Again, this is situation-specific care, not some indefinite attribute called LOVE. We need repentance. When our conscience is receptive to correction, not defensive, such conviction shows the Spirit's hand. Not SIN in general, but for these my sins, Lord, have mercy on me. We need faith. When we find ourselves alive to truth and relating honestly to God in joy, or need, or thanks, we are receiving what we have asked. Again, not some generic quality of FAITH, but living, specific faith.

LESSON EIGHT

PUT THE WORD TO WORK

I. THE VALUE OF A WRITTEN SYSTEM
(It is more fun and engaging to not play the first part of this video tape and do this first point interactively.)

Q. *How many here use a pocket calendar to stay organized? A palm pilot? A wall calendar at home? Who has no calendar? (I ask for a show of hands for each one.)*

Q. *Why do we almost all have calendars? We forget.*

Q. *What happens if we forget? Miss appointments.*

Q. *What's so bad about missing appointments? Waste time. Get embarrassed. Waste money. Never get anything done.*

Q. *How many people here have a method of writing down their prayer requests that they use regularly? (I have them put their heads down and raise their hands. I apologize for making them feel like 8th graders, but I don't want people to feel awkward.)*

Q. Why do so many more of us have a personal calendar but so few of us have a written prayer system?

- *We don't know how to do it.*
- *Don't place same value on it.*
- *Don't see consequences immediately.*
- *Don't care.*
- *Seems unnatural to have everything written down.*
- *We don't believe that prayer really works.*

II. PRAYER ASSUMES AN UNSEEN CONNECTEDNESS IN LIFE

- *Littleton, CO just after the shootings of 13 students. What were people doing? Praying, praying in closets, in hallways, praying for the school. Is there a connection between forbidding prayer in public schools and violence?*
- *Enlightenment. Fog descended on Western civilization 200 years ago and it has slowly been getting thicker. Ignores the spiritual world.*
- *Peter Jennings to ABC reporters, "When you ask someone, 'What got you through this crisis?' and they say, 'God', don't say, 'No, what really got you through?'"*

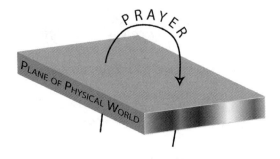

PRAYER ASSUMES AN UNSEEN CONNECTEDNESS

III. WHY A WRITTEN SYSTEM?

* We are disabled when it comes to prayer—face your disability, don't deny it.
  ~ *Antenna is broken.*
  ~ *We are stroke victims in the prayer part of our brain.*
  ~ *Disabled need adaptations: speech computers, wheel chairs, TTY.*
* Benefits to writing:
  ~ *Able to remember the prayer request.*
  ~ *Able to watch what God does over a period of time, begin to see the pattern, the story of what God is doing.*
  ~ *Helps me concentrate on them, remember their needs.*
  ~ *Encourages me to pray more. "Wow, when Jesus said, 'ask me anything and I will do it for you,' he really meant it."*
  ~ *Story of "Put the Word to Work."*

[One of my children]

* With xxxxxx—"Accept one another, then just as Christ accepted you in order to bring praise to God."
* How do I disciple him/her?
* Math, Reading, Science, S.S., and Bible
* Honesty "put away all deceit"
* Basketball, track
* Friends, good friends that love Jesus
* Psalm 51 "you desire truth in the inward parts"
* Know and walk with Jesus

Q. What patterns do you see? (Brainstorm)
  - *Use Scripture.*
- *Every part of this child's life is being prayed for. "Ask anything."*
- *Questions that I leave unanswered.*
- *Each one of these requests has turned into a story. These stories almost always involve me. Some really dramatic answers to prayer.*
- *Always surprising.*
- *Begin to expect God to do things. It really becomes fascinating. "What will God do next?"*

A new way of seeing relational change. A lot of times words do not work. In all of Christian writing on relationships very little is said about prayer.

V. STUDY FROM THE SERMON ON THE MOUNT
- Look at it through grid of power in relationships.
  - ~ *Jesus' ministry and in particular the Sermon on the Mount (Matt 5-7) are about giving up power.*
  - ~ *The Sermon on the Mount is like a room where Jesus slowly closes all the doors to the human exercise of power.*

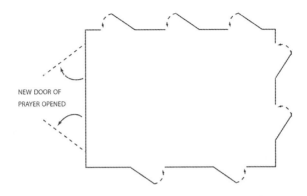

NEW DOOR OF
PRAYER OPENED

~ *Matt. 5:5, "The meek shall inherit the earth." Humble yourself in relationships.*

~ *5:38-47, empower your enemies, those who abuse you. Taking away wrong use of power.*

~ *6:1, keep your devotion to God slightly hidden so you don't use it to make yourself look good. Don't use spirituality as a means for getting power. Takes away power in spiritual life, by actively hiding your righteousness.*

☐ *If you fast, pretend you aren't.*

☐ *If you pray, do it in private.*

☐ *If you give, don't tell anyone.*

~ *6:19, lose power by giving.*

Ugh! Who's going to take care of me?

~ *6:25, your heavenly Father will! Give up worrying!*

~ *7:1, when someone else has sinned, lose power bu instead of using that information to correct them, use that information to humble yourself by first finding the beam in your own eye.*

• *New Way of Power: 7:7, "Ask."*

  ~ *He opens a door that we have left closed.*

  ~ *A new way of getting things done.*

PRAYER ASSIGNMENT:
Write up some cards for people in your life. See Appendix A for Scriptures to help you.

THE LORD'S PRAYER | By putting the Word to work, we are taking prayer seriously as a functional part of our daily life, along with eating, sleeping, etc. We are entering into the mind of God where his name, his kingdom, and his will rule.

David Powlison's Reflections

When you pray, push yourself past the obvious and external. We usually aks God to change events in people's lives: health for the sick, to get a job, and so forth. But think about the spiritual needs in each of these life situations. Is this sick person fearful of death, as well as sick? Is this mother angry at her straying teen, as well as wanting the stray to be found? Does this man define his meaning through his work? Does he need to grow in finding identity in his God, along with needing a job? Does your pastor need to be delivered from people-pleasing, as well as to preach the truth well? Pray not only for circumstantial blessings, but also for what God is changing in the person through the circumstance.

LESSON NINE

PRAYER WORK

I. THE STORY OF J. O. FRASER IN SOUTHWESTERN CHINA

- *Beginnings.*
  - ~ *CIM started by Hudson Taylor.*
  - ~ *Just before WWI Fraser was sent to SW China, drawn to Lisu people.*
  - ~ *Mountainous region with steep valleys and deep gorges.*
  - ~ *Initial flurry of conversions, then slipping back.*
  - ~ *The idols were too powerful.*
- *Learning to Pray.*
  - ~ *Began to pray and recruit prayer. Wrote letters, prayer circles.*
  - ~ *Praying for villages.*
  - ~ *Prayer for the priest at the sword ladder festival.*
  - ~ *Likened prayer to a farmer in the west who receives a claim from the government. That is the prayer. Now he has to work the claim for ten years to receive permanent title.*

- *Final Letter.*
  - ~ *After five years wrote a letter to Mr. Hoste, the Director of CIM, "Please reassign me. This isn't working."*
  - ~ *He had a good reason: the reality of God's work among the Lisu did not equal his hope. To have not requested re-assignment would have been denial.*
  - ~ *God changed Fraser through the waiting, but he was also concerned for the Lisu. He was waiting for the threads of the story to come together.*
- *Final Trip.*
  - ~ *Before he mailed the letter requesting reassignment, he decided to take one more trip.*
  - ~ *First village he presented the gospel almost completely without passion. He wanted no human manipulation. "Here is the truth. You need to follow it."*
  - ~ *Young Lisu father and son traveling with him, "Teacher, wait a little. Two families want to turn Christian if we will help them."*
  - ~ *Melting Pot—ten families, Cypress Hill—15 families, Turtle Village—24 families, Mottled Hill—49 families. By the end of the trip there were 129 families, 600 conversions.*
  - ~ *Now, 120,000 Lisu Christians in Burma and China.*

II. EXAMPLE OF PRAYER CARDS USED IN WORK SETTING:

BOOK ON JESUS
How do it with Anita?
How much?
When time to redo 1?
When time to redo 2 and 3?
Intro letter?
When pursue publisher?
How balance with all my other work?
Which publisher?
When do I have time to learn to write?
Father, I pray NavPress would say "yes".
Give me wisdom how to re-write it.

LOVE IN BALANCE [Feeding of 5,000]

Does story of Jill and I fit with Feeding of 5,000?
When do I end the Feeding of the 5,000?
Is chap necessary?
Is Feeding of 5,000 best used with 4 kinds of will?
Am I forcing the chapter into mold of 4 kinds of will?
Am I wise to drop the story of the boat?
Is 5,000 more on faith?
How do I write on this? Bring prayer material up?

[PASTOR IN MARYLAND]   **Frederick, MD**

3 groups started — October 10th
10/99 5 non-Christians
      Joe-Suicidal
      Susie and Bob-military couple
      Melanie-military
      Trish-a woman who is seeking answers
10/99 George and Janet living together
      Barb-40's, cancer
11/99 Barb became a Christian!

PRAYER ASSIGNMENT: Think through one project at work (or home if you don't work outside the home) that you are struggling with and write down some of the questions you have. Choose a Scripture that you can use to help you pray for that project. Then pray using the card. See Appendix A for Scripture to help you.

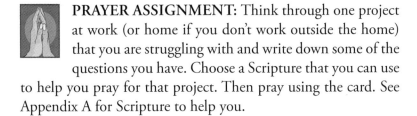

THE LORD'S PRAYER

By slowing down and praying over our work, we are taking a stand against our culture's tendency to privatize spirituality. We don't just pray for sick people. We pray for everything. By praying over our work, we bring God's kingdom and rule into our work lives.

David Powlison's Reflections

It's with good reason that the Lord's Prayer features "Hallowed be your name, your kingdom come, your will be done on earth as it is in heaven." That zeroes in on God revealing himself on the stage of real-time human history. Often his name is disregarded, not hallowed. Many competing powers-that-be parade across the stage of history. God's stated will is often ignored or openly opposed. So prayers that long for the open revelation of God as king are prayers aligned with his central purpose. And since this King works in real life through real people, our projects count. When you pray for your work, the ministries of your church, or for the ministry of a friend, you are praying that God will reveal a bit of his kingdom here and now.

LESSON TEN

THANKING GOD

I. WE LIVE IN A WORLD OF UNBELIEF UNLIKE ANY OTHER WORLD THAT EXISTED BEFORE.

- How does unbelief express itself?
  Examples: Dan Rather doesn't open the news with prayer. (Not advocating a return to Christendom. I just mean that every newscaster should begin bowing his head and saying, "God we ate your food, breathed your air, and enjoyed life today. Thank-you." That is why the Muslim world hates the west. They correctly discern and fear our godless materialism.
- Thanklessness is inherent in losing our perspective.

Q. How does unbelief express itself? Romans 1:18-21. What is the first sin that comes out?
  ~ *Thanklessness.*
  ~ *Thanklessness is inherent in losing perspective. We lost perspective and took God out of the center of the universe. There was no one to thank.*

II. THANKING GOD IN PRAYER

- Reviewing your day/week just ruminating on the goodness of God.
  - ~ *Restores the sanity that this world takes away.*
  - ~ *Helps you to stay in touch with God's ongoing story in your life.*
  - ~ *Fun to do. Little details will come to mind of how God provided.*
  - ~ *Naturally leads to worship.*
- Specific prayer cards where you list how God is good to you in giving you this person.
  - ~ *Our view of people close to us gets unbalanced because of our hearts. Thanking God for them restores the sanity of these people as a gift to us.*
  - ~ *Be specific. Example of prayers of thanks for a spouse: "organized, pretty, hard working, good cook, keeps the house clean, loves the kids...."*
  - ~ *Not asking you to deny the other person's faults, just see them in the context of God's gift to you.*
  - ~ *When you reach for the soap in the shower and realize it isn't there because of some quirk of your spouse start going through your list while you are gritting your teeth. Restore your sanity.*

PRAYER ASSIGNMENT:
1) Review your day. Just reflect on God's goodness to you. Maybe review the week. 2) Write out a prayer card on one person in your life and how you are thankful for them. See Appendix A for Scripture to help you.

The Lord's Prayer begins with hallowing God's name. Thanking God involves taking our eyes off ourselves and seeing the greatness and goodness of God.

David Powlison's Reflection on *Thanking God* can be seen on page 92.

Lesson Ten: *Thanking God*

LESSON ELEVEN

REPENTANCE AND INTERCESSORY PRAYING

I. REFLECTING ON PRAYER AND REPENTANCE

Each of us has besetting sins that are "the dark side" of our personality. Repentance praying is just reviewing one of those sins to ask the Holy Spirit's help today with that particular tendency.

II. REPENTANCE: "WARNING TO MY FLESH"

As you slow down you'll recall something you did or said that was motivated by self. Just simply acknowledge that to God.

> **PRUDENCE-TONGUE**
> If I have been hurt by someone, I want to relieve the pressure by talking about them.
>
> Psalm 34:12,13
> "Whoever of you loves life and desires to see many good days, keep your tongue from evil and your lips from speaking lies."

> **WAITING**
> Rushing to fill the position of _____ with _____ in _____
>
> Proverbs 14:8
> "The wisdom of the prudent is to give thought to their ways."

III. PEOPLE IN NEED CARD

> **PEOPLE IN NEED CARD**
> Isaiah 61:1-3
> "The Spirit of the Sovereign Lord is on me, because the Lord has anointed me...to comfort all who mourn and provide for those who grieve in Zion—to bestow on them a crown of beauty instead of ashes, the oil of gladness instead of mourning, and a garment of praise instead of a spirit of despair."
> [names of kids who've left the faith]
>
> Mom/Jill
> Dan and Betty Herron
> Gabe/Barb/Angelo

IV. OTHER CARDS
* Friends.
* Small Group.
* Non-Christians.
* Promise/Hope.

V. POWER OF PRAYER

Babushkas: Word on the street in Moscow, "Communism's great mistake was in ignoring the Babushkas. They went after the youth, but the praying old women were the ones who brought communism down."

 PRAYER ASSIGNMENT: Complete your stack of cards by adding additional categories from this video. See Appendix A to help you.

SAMPLE STACK OF CARDS: (This is a suggested list only. Customize your set of cards for your burdens and your life.)

* 4-10 Family Cards (one card for each person).
* 1-3 People Suffering Cards.
* 1 Friends Card.
* 1 Non-Christian Card.
* 1 My Church's Leadership (pastor, elders, etc).
* 1-3 My Small Group.
* 1 Missionary, Service Work.
* 1-3 World Issues, Things that burden me.
* 1 Co-Workers.
* 1-3 Work Cards (projects or problems at work).
* 3-4 Repentance Cards.
* 3-4 Hope Cards.

Being with God in prayer leads very naturally to repentance praying to "forgive us our sins." It flows so naturally out of prayer because repentance is just seeing yourself from God's point of view. That is what you are doing in prayer.

David Powlison's Reflections

My favorite prayer of confession is Psalm 25. David asks the Lord first to forgive him and second to keep teaching him to become different. "Be of sin the double cure, cleanse me of its guilt and power," as the old hymn captured it. The most radical, freeing line of comes midpoint in verse 11: "For your name's sake, O Lord, pardon my iniquity, for it is great." Think about that. Forgive, for your name's sake. Forgive me because of who you are. That is a radical confidence in God's character, promises, and grace. When you pray that way, you are asking God to forgive you based entirely on who he is, and completely contrary to who you are on your own. "Remember yourself when you look at me, Lord. Remember what you are like, and don't remember me in and of myself." In fact, throughout the whole psalm, David does this over and over. He asks God to remember his promise of compassion, his goodness, and not to remember David's sins. Do have any tendencies to get stuffed up within yourself after you've failed and are feeling guilty? This psalm is freedom!

APPENDIX

SCRIPTURE FOR YOUR CARDS

- When you are praying for someone, use Scripture that describes what you want to happen in their lives.
- When you or someone you are praying for is in a difficult situation, use Scripture that looks to God's deliverance, in his time.
- The "Repentance" verses are meant for you (or someone else) who has a besetting sin. Use Scripture that describes the new habit of the heart that you want to see God work in your life (or the other person).
- This is not magic. You are simply taking God's thoughts and praying them back to him. Pray that God would lead you to the right Scripture.

BLESSING
3 John 2

CHILDREN, OBEDIENCE
Ephesians 6:1

CHILDREN, PROMISES
Isaiah 38:19; 49:25; 59:21; 65:23

CHILDREN, LOST
Isaiah 43:6; 49:12; 60:4

COMFORT
Psalm 23

DELIGHT IN ANOTHER
PERSON
Philippians 4:8
I Thessalonians 1:2
II Timothy 1:4

DIRECTION
Isaiah 42:16; 45:3; 52:12

DIVORCED, LONELY
Isaiah 54:4

GUILT
Isaiah 40:2; 44:22
Psalm 103:12; 130:3,4

IMPOSSIBLE SITUATIONS
Isaiah 41:10
Habakkuk 3:17-19

FAITH
Matthew 17:19-21
Mark 9:22-24
Luke 22:32
John 20:27
Romans 4:19,20, 11:20, 12:2
II Corinthians 11:3
Hebrews 11:1,6

FORGIVENESS, FORBEARANCE
Romans 15:7
Ephesians 4:2
Colossians 3:12,13
I Peter 4:8

LOST, UNCONVERTED FRIENDS
OR FAMILY
Isaiah 52:7, 10
Psalm 57:5

MARRIAGE
Isaiah 62:4

MONEY/FINANCE
Proverbs 3:9-10
Proverbs 6:6-8
Matthew 6:19-24
Mark 12:43-44
Luke 12:15
Romans 8:32
2 Corinthians 9:6-11

PASSION FOR GOD
Psalm 27:4, 37:4, 63:1

PROMISE, HOPE, MERCY
Isaiah 42:6,7, 45:2,3, 55:1
Habakkuk 3:2
Romans 8:37-39, 15:13

PROTECTION
Psalm 32:6, 7; 35; 91; 121
Isaiah 43:2

REPENTANCE: ANGER
Proverbs 12:16, 14:29,
15:18, 19:11, 20:3,
Ephesians 4:26,31,32

REPENTANCE: APPROVAL SEEKING
Galatians 1:10
John 5:41, 42, 44

REPENTANCE: AUTHORITY
Philippians 2:15
Colossians 3:17

REPENTANCE: BITTERNESS
Hebrews 12:15

REPENTANCE: COLDNESS
OR LACK OF WARMTH
I Thessalonians 1:8, 2:17, 3:6,9,10

REPENTANCE: COMPLAINING
Philippians 2:14,15
Colossians 3:17

REPENTANCE: CRITICAL
Romans 15:7

REPENTANCE: DECEIT
Ephesians 4:25

REPENTANCE: DYING TO SELF,
TO PLANS, TO CONTROL
Mark 8:34-38
John 12:23-26

REPENTANCE: HUMILITY
Romans 12:3,16
Ephesians 4:2
Philippians 2:1-3
I Peter 5:5,6
James 4:6-10

REPENTANCE: IDOLS
Isaiah 50:11

REPENTANCE: JUDGING
Matthew 7:1-5
I Corinthians 4:3

REPENTANCE: LAZINESS
Proverbs 26;14

REPENTANCE: LISTENING TO REBUKE
Proverbs 12:1; 13:1;
15:5,10,12,31,32

REPENTANCE: LOVE OF
MONEY, GREED
Matthew 6:19-24
I Timothy 6:17
I John 2:15-17

REPENTANCE: QUIET SPIRIT
Isaiah 30:15

REPENTANCE: PATIENCE
Ephesians 4:2

REPENTANCE: PRUDENCE
WITH "TONGUE CONTROL"
Proverbs 10:8,14,19; 11:12,13;
12:23; 17:28; 18:13; 20:19;
21:23; 24:28; 29:20
Psalm 34:12,13
Ephesians 4:29

REPENTANCE: PRUDENCE
WITH FRIENDSHIP
Proverbs 12:26

REPENTANCE: REVENGE,
RETALIATION
Deuteronomy 32:35
Proverbs 20:22
Romans 12:17
I Thessalonians 5:15
I Peter 2:23, 3:9

REPENTANCE: SEXUAL LUST
Psalm 51:6, 7, 10
Proverbs 7:7-9, 25, 27
I Peter 1:14

REPENTANCE: SELF-CONFIDENCE
Proverbs 3:5
James 4:13-16

REPENTANCE: SELF-RIGHTEOUSNESS
I Peter 3:18
Luke 10:29

REPENTANCE: SELF-WILL
Psalm 19:13
John 4:34, 5:19, 6:38,
7:6,16,28, 8:28,42, 12:49,50

REPENTANCE: WAITING
Isaiah 30:1,15
Proverbs 14:8

REPENTANCE, WAITING
IN SUFFERING
Psalm 37:7
Lamentations 3:19-26

REPENTANCE: WORRY
Matthew 6:25-34

STRESS
Matthew 11: 28-30
I Peter 5:7, 10-11

SPOUSE
Micah 6:8
I Peter 3:1-7
Ephesians 4:22-32

SUFFERING
Psalm 34:18
Isaiah 40:30,31

Romans 5:3-5
I Peter 4:12,13; 5:10
Hebrews 10:36
James 1:2,3,12

SICKNESS & HEALING
Isaiah 61:1-3
Psalm 116

WEARY, BEAT DOWN
Isaiah 40:28-31

WORK
Ephesians 6:7,8
Colossians 3:17,22-24

WORK, WORKING WITH
DIFFICULT PEOPLE
Daniel 4:37

APPENDIX

LISTENING TO GOD
IN PRAYER

A number of years ago, I took a retreat day in December to pray through my goals for the year. During longer times of prayer such as this, I meditate and pray through passages of Scripture. Sometimes I am simply still before God...slowing down so I can become more aware of the direction of my life, my thoughts, and my heart. Where have I been too busy? What is God doing?

This morning I prayed, "What do you want me to focus on? How do you want me to focus?" The thought came to me, "I don't want you to have any goals this year. I'm going to work on your character." I wondered what character issues I should work on. Again, a simple thought came to me, "You know. It's obvious." And it was. I started to reflect on the issues that God had been dealing with me over the last several years and almost immediately a list of seven items came to mind. Under the topic "God's Heart for Paul," I wrote: waiting and prayer, listening and patience with people, relaxing with people, cultivating humility, quiet heart before you, prudence and dignity, and unashamed of Jesus in witnessing.

Now here's the question: Was God in some way speaking to me during that day of prayer or was it just my own thoughts? Did the Spirit prompt me or was it just my intuition? My answer is a qualified "yes." It was the Spirit prompting me. In order to understand both my "yes" and my "qualifications," I need to tell you what happened that year.

Six weeks later, my work and my ministry literally fell apart. It was the hardest year of my life. If I'd used that day in December to write my goals instead of praying, it would have been an exercise in futility. God did nothing that year but work on my character! Each of those seven areas became a little story that was being shaped by God through suffering. Let me explain by looking at just one of those seven issues: a burden for the lost.

Shortly before my prayer retreat, I'd asked my father who was also my boss how he'd like me to improve in my work. He replied, "I'd like you to have more of a burden for the lost." Internally, I bristled at Dad's answer, because for 13 years he and I had worked side-by-side growing our mission to 90 missionaries. As Associate Director, few had done more in reaching the lost than I. But I knew that wasn't what Dad was talking about. He wanted me *personally* to have more of a concern for non-Christians. *Personally*, witnessing intimidated me. Growing up in a Christian home and going to Christian schools, I was not used to non-Christians. So I began to pray that God would give me a greater burden for the lost.

Four months later in April, I was praying again while walking along the Mediterranean in Spain. My heart was heavy because Dad was not recovering from open-heart surgery. I knew he was dying. As I walked along the wharf, numb, I thought again of my Dad's burden for the lost, and I prayed that God would give me my Dad's burden and multiply it. A month later, I nervously began my first *Person of Jesus* Bible study with a small group of non-Christians. My friend, Paul Osborne, had called me after Dad's funeral and asked me if I wanted to postpone the study. I said, "No, Dad would have wanted me to do it." Now years later, I've written a book and a Bible study for non-Christians. I get almost daily emails from people who are sharing Christ with non-Christians through these tools.

Does God speak to us with a personal touch, prompt us to obey and love? Yes. Does he intimately personalize his counsel and power to each of us in each of our situations, or his counsel in Scripture only generally to all of us? I believe, with several qualifications, that God does personalize his counsel to us. Our Father works as a personal vinedresser in our lives.

My first "qualification" to my "yes" is that surrounding that December prayer was a story saturated with God's Word. The most obvious is Christ's burden for the lost. But notice also the Biblical themes of humility and repentance. When I had bristled internally at my Dad, I thought, "Paul, you are just proud. What's wrong with turning his request into a prayer? There is truth in it." So instead of hiding behind my "record" as Associate Director, I began to pray that I would have a love for non-Christians. Then later, I prayed like Elisha for a portion of Elijah's spirit. The Word shaped the content, motivation, and structure of my prayer just as it had shaped the content and motivation of my Dad's words to me. That December prayer time fit perfectly with the unfolding story of the Spirit's work in my life as he used the Word to shape my heart. You can easily see the hand of the divine gardener pruning one of his branches (John 15).

Without God's Word, there is no authority shaping the unfolding story. Unless the Bible guards and directs our intuitions, we can run amok and baptize our selfish desires with religious language ("God told me to marry her…"). Keeping the Word and the Spirit together is the key to making sure that 'God-talk' doesn't become a cover for my own desires.

Here's a further qualification. I believe the Spirit was behind the scenes at every point in the story: when I asked my dad how he'd like me to improve, when my dad said he'd like me to have a burden for the lost, when I prayed in December, when I prayed in Spain, and when I started *The Person of Jesus* study. At every point the Spirit was directing and shaping. Each qualifies as "low-level divine communication." It is not necessary to elevate one part of the Spirit's directing above another. We expect the Spirit to use circumstances, creation, other Christians,

---

and the Word to awaken and guide us. Consequently, I am cautious using the language "God spoke to me" for that December morning because I don't want to elevate my intuitions above the multitude of ways that God has to continually communicate with us.

For example, I believe God was "speaking" to me when my Dad encouraged me to have more of a burden for the lost. That same was true when I reflected, "Paul, you are just proud. ..." That is a Spirit-directed insight into my sinful tendencies. God is personalizing his words to me. The Bible repeatedly encourages us to have thoughts like that ("Humble yourself under the might hand of God"). If we dignify one form of God's "intuitive" Spirit-directed communication over another, we can undermine the authority of God's Word. And yet at the same time, I think it is proper to say it was God "speaking"—just so you apply that uniformly to the rest of the incidents in that story.

Another way to have gone wrong with that December prayer time would be to elevate it to the level of Biblical authoritative communication by stopping my work (since I wasn't supposed to have goals) and waiting for the "fulfillment" of the prophecy. I didn't. I actually forgot about it until the year started getting hard. Or, I could have elevated it by telling other people about it. I didn't. In fact, I didn't mention it to anyone until several years later. It was a personal word for me that gave meaning and hope during a hard year. It wasn't something to build my life on; it was just a kind word from my heavenly Father.

When referring to our communication with God, the Bible prefers to emphasize our listening instead of God speaking. The focus is more on my heart surrendered than on the means of communication. Am I attentive to God? Is my heart soft and teachable? Am I remembering his ways, his commands? (Psalm 25:15, "My eyes are ever on the Lord.") Otherwise, there is a tendency to interrupt the story line in the middle by jumping to the end of the play in order to tell how the story is going to come out—as if you were the playwright. My responsibility as a believer is to cultivate a listening heart in the midst of the cacophony of noise from my own heart and from the world—not to mention the devil. To lock in and say, "God spoke to me this morning," can suggest

I have an inside track on how the story will come out. I always want to remember that I am simply an actor on God's stage where every line is his—not just some of them.

When people frequently call their intuition "God speaking," it has several potential dangers: First, it can cheapen God speaking in the same way that the shepherd crying "wolf" does for the villagers. Secondly, by making "God speaking" commonplace, God is hard to hear when he does speak. Thirdly, it also subtly puts you in control of God by opening the door to your voice being equal with God's voice—since God's voice and your own desires come in on the same channel. It undermines God's Word by functionally elevating human intuition to the status of divine revelation. My wife Jill and I have a running joke about her "being led" into antique stores. She'll say, "Paul, I don't know what came over me, but it was like someone else was turning the steering wheel into the parking lot." Right. I've done the same with a new venture in the ministry where I've launched out because I was sure this was would help us, but it really was a combination of idolatry and self-will.

Finally, referring often to "God speaking" can create a false, elevated spirituality as if someone who hears a lot from God is more spiritual. Paul the Apostle mixes his language when talking about his plans. At times, he speaks of God's leading, but more frequently, he just talks about his own desires and plans. To be blunt, when you frequently confuse human intuition and God's communicating, you get weird. Distortion always comes with pride.

Having reflected on the dangers of deifying human intuition, I want to look more positively at that December prayer time. I believe that December prayer time was what I've called "God's intuitive Spirit-directed communication" or "low-level divine communication." Why do I think that?

First, as we've already seen, my question in prayer and subsequent answer were immersed in personal reflections on and obedience to God's Word. It was just one stage in an unfolding Biblically-informed story of repentance in my life. It was the exact opposite of human intuition gone amok. In fact, my human intuition was being mastered by God. Psalm 25:14, "The Lord confides in those who fear him; he makes his covenant known to them."

My second observation is the unusual character of my reflections that morning. I was completely surprised by the thought, "I don't want you to have goals this year." It came entirely out of the blue. I'm almost obsessive about goals—I'd never had a thought like that before. And strikingly, it came true. In the Bible, we see the same surprising quality to God's intervention. Who would have guessed that God would become man, die in our place, and rise again?

The larger context of my life is also helpful. God seldom "speaks" to me this overtly. Usually, I discern God's will as the Holy Spirit through a combination of circumstances, his Word, and other Christians. An example is the prayers that are written on the cover of the A Praying Life manual, which I journaled just before seminary. All of them were answered over the period of the next few years in remarkable ways but largely through circumstances. I find that same pattern in the lives of other Christians and in Paul the Apostle's life as well. On several occasions, particularly during difficult times, Paul will get a special message from God as he did at Corinth (Acts 18:9,10), but that seems to be rare even for Paul.

Earlier, we looked at the danger of the actor in the drama (me) taking the role of the playwright (God). But there is also the danger of missing the play entirely. If you focus exclusively on God's written Word without a heart that is listening to him speak directly into your life, then you'll miss the unfolding story of his work. You'll miss seeing the patterns of the divine artist etching the character of his Son on your heart. Consequently, your Christian life will tend to be dull, lacking the sparkle and immediacy of God's presence. If I hadn't taken the time that December morning to pray and put my questions before God, the following year would have lacked some of the rich meaning and fellowship with God.

If I am to be a good sheep, I need to develop an eye for the shepherd, to be able to read his face. I need to develop a poet's eye that can read the patterns in my Father's good creation (Psalm 19). Like a good story-teller I need to pick up the cadence and heart-beat of the Divine Story-Teller. I need to tune in to my Father's voice above the noise of my own heart and the surrounding world, what C.S. Lewis calls the "kingdom of noise."

The application of God's Word to your life is greatly enhanced when you see God's activity in the details of your life. You actually undermine the impact of God's Word in your life by defining God's speaking too narrowly. If the Psalms are the pouring out of man's heart to God, then Isaiah is the pouring out of God's heart to man. We need to be in tune with both patterns. We need to guard against rationalism and scholasticism as much as we need to guard against emotionalism and experientialism.

We've already seen that we can separate the activity of listening to God from obedience to God's Word. This happens when we let human intuition run amok by using "God words" to provide cover for what we want to do. What we "hear" from God appears like obedience when, in fact, it is just masking our self-will. But hearing and obedience can also be separated by simply focusing on obedience and ignoring listening. Listening to and obeying God are so intertwined in Biblical thought that they are one word in the Hebrew, *shamar*.

Those thoughts that came to my mind that December were not in any sense a new divine authoritative revelation. They were simply an extended, personal application of the Word to my life in the coming year. Practically, they helped me focus, so that when suffering came I immediately began to think of God's desire to work on my character. It gave the year meaning and hope. It was not unlike what Jesus told Peter at the Last Supper when he said, "You will deny me three times." Later when Jesus turned and looked at Peter after his third denial, Jesus' pointed warning would have brought him more quickly to a deeper repentance. It would unmasked his heart...which is how repentance begins. It gave Peter hope, possibly saving Peter from suicide. "Jesus knew this about me ahead of time and yet he loved me still. In fact he prayed for me that I wouldn't despair."

To summarize, there are two dangers in "God spoke to me". The first danger (a form of Romanticism) absolutizes my feelings. Under the cover of "being led by the Spirit" we can easily just do what we want. The second danger (a form of Rationalism) absolutizes our thinking. Under the cover of being obedient to the Word, we can be rigid. We need both the Word and the Spirit. We need the sharp edged, absolute character of the Word and the intuitive, personal leading of the Spirit. The Word shows us how the Spirit leads us from the rigidity of legalism, and the Spirit shows us how the Word brings the clarity of obedience. The Spirit uses the Word in our life, and the Word comes alive as applied by the Spirit.

It is difficult to precisely define listening to God. The interaction between the divine Spirit and our own spirits is mysterious (particularly in our modern rationalistic age). David captures this mystery in Psalm 16:7, "I bless the Lord who gives me counsel; in the night also my heart instructs me." The intuitive nature of this communication is reflected in how the psalmist parallels "the Lord who gives me counsel" with "my heart (literally "my gut") instructs me". So what happened? Was David's heart talking to him or was God giving him counsel? The two are impossible to separate. It has a hard-to-pin-down-but-nevertheless-real quality. We can only approximate it and observe some of its characteristics. Our fallenness and finitude means that we don't have the mental capacity to adequately analyze this kind of interaction. You can never channel it or compartmentalize it. The counsel God gives David is inseparable from David's active pursuit of God: "I have set the Lord always before me…" (16:8). The counsel from God doesn't function like a talisman or a fortune teller, because it is inseparable from a humble seeking after God. ❧

"Prayer in the sense of petition, asking for things, is a small part of it (prayer); confession and penitence are its threshold, adoration its sanctuary, the presence and vision and enjoyment of God its bread and wine." —C. S. Lewis

APPENDIX C

"LECTIO DIVINA"
Divine Reading

This is an ancient practice that began nearly 1600 years ago with the Desert Fathers. It is a devotional reading of God's Word to help one draw near to God, listen to him, be more conformed to his will. It is a way to "let the word of Christ dwell richly within you." Thomas Watson, a 17th century Puritan, said "Let the Scriptures not only inform you but also inflame you."

SILENCE. Find a quiet spot and settle down, relax.

READING. Slowly read the text aloud. There is no hurry, so do not try to rush through it.

MEDITATION. When you come to a word or phrase that seems to speak to you, repeat it slowly again and again. Reflect on its meaning. Let the text sink deep into your heart. You may even wish to imagine in your mind's eye the event or scene.

PRAYING. What does God seem to be saying to you? How does

your heart respond? Open your heart to God in whatever way is appropriate: thanksgiving, longing, joy, sadness, etc. Be honest with your thoughts, feelings, and desire before God.

RESTING. Quietly sit in God's presence, rest in his arms.

Take 10-15 minutes, or longer to do this.

David Powlison's Reflections

In giving thanks, connect little daily things with the biggest things about the Lord. For example, how many times have you said grace before a meal in a rote manner? How does this meal connect to the God of heaven and earth?! I've found that simply pausing and slowing down helps me mean the words I say. It helps me to remember the God I'm thanking, as well as the particulars for which I'm thankful. Think before you thank, and think as you thank.

Here's an example. "Thank you, Father, that you have given us this food tonight…. [Saying it slower than normal helps it sink in. For a moment, reflect about what you've just said. You'll view the food differently. Perhaps you'll begin thinking about what it means that you have a Father who gives.] Thank you that you are our Father… and that we are experiencing your kindness today… and thank you that Jesus is your best kindness to us." An 8-second prayer taking 13 seconds can mean the difference between routine and reality.

ABOUT THE AUTHOR

After graduating from Temple University in 1975, Paul taught in inner city Christian schools in Philadelphia for ten years. He was the founding principal at Spruce Hill Christian School, an inner city, multi-racial school.

In 1983 he helped his father, Dr. Jack Miller, found World Harvest Mission, and served as Associate Director from 1983-96. During that time Paul wrote the *Sonship* course, *Discipling by Grace* (the precursor to *Gospel Transformation*), and *The Love Course*. In 1999 he completed an M.Div. at Biblical Seminary. During those years Paul was a deacon and elder at New Life Church, Glenside, PA.

Paul founded seeJesus in 1999, a discipling mission. In 2001, Paul wrote *Love Walked Among Us* (NavPress), a companion book to *The Person of Jesus* study (2002). In 2005, the *A Praying Life Study* was released followed by *A Praying Life* (NavPress, 2009). The *Ruth* study was released in 2011. In 2014, Paul's latest book, *A Loving Life* (Crossway, 2014) was released. SeeJesus' mission is to help people see and reflect the life, death and resurrection of Jesus through its discipleship resources and training.

Paul is married to Jill, who is known for her sense of humor and faith. They have six children and eight grandchildren.

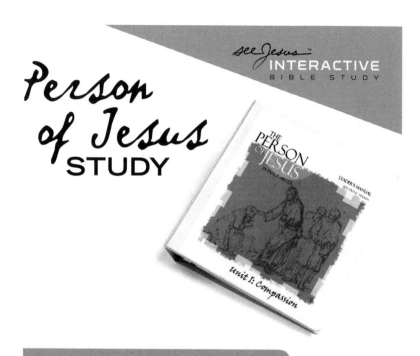

Person of Jesus STUDY

How do you love without feeling trapped or used?

How do you balance honesty with compassion?

How do you love when you have problems of your own?

Suitable for discipling or evangelism, *The Person of Jesus* study introduces a Christ so personal, so rich in love that participants are captivated heart-first. Bill, a study leader in Orlando, said, "I've never seen anything like this! I'm enjoying this study as much as a new believer!"

Whether you are looking for a study to invite friends to, or a study for your small groups at church, this is a great tool. Its interactive style engages all participants in a non-threatening way. Designed for first-time through seasoned leaders, this study offers an easy-to-use format, saturated with in-depth content.

To purchase your copy, visit our website at
www.seeJesus.net, or call 215-721-3113

A LOVING LIFE

Interactive Bible Study

(formerly titled,
Ruth: Love Redefined)

A loving life is what we all want. But loving people is hard. Drawing on the book of Ruth, *A Loving Life* offers the help we need to embrace relationship, endure rejection, cultivate community, and reach out to even the most unlovable around us as we discover the power to live a loving life.

Book

(published by Crossway,
January 2014)

"Through the biblical story of Ruth, Paul gives us hope, not hype—the freedom to suffer well, stay present, and live expectantly in all of our relationships." –SCOTTY SMITH, TEACHER-IN-RESIDENCE, WEST END COMMUNITY CHURCH, NASHVILLE, TN

To purchase your copy, visit our website at
www.seeJesus.net, or call 215-721-3113